"There is so much more to marriage than meets the eye; our relationships on earth have the potential to help us understand a much larger reality. Ryan Messmore points to this bigger story, and in so doing, he helps us develop a deeper understanding of the gifts of sex and marriage. For college students wrestling with questions about human sexuality and relationships, for couples preparing for marriage, or for any of us wanting to see how our real-life relationships can point to a much deeper spiritual reality, this book is a treasure trove of insight and inspiration."
-D. Michael Lindsay, President, Gordon College, United States

"Every love story is really an epic waiting to be told. Ryan Messmore shows us how he discovered that epic dimension in the divine. He discovered God's action in the small details of his relationship with his wife Karin, and their love began to flourish in unexpected ways. This is more than another intellectual conversion story. It's a romance. It's theology. It's the kind of story that changes all kinds of lives for the better."
–Scott Hahn, professor of theology, Franciscan University of Steubenville, United States

"If love is not forever, what's forever for? Ryan and Karin's story shows how our deepest human longing can be made beautiful, fresh, compelling and highly realistic—even in the age of the hook-up culture. *In Love* is a love story that opens up a brighter prospect for our generation."
-Os Guinness, author of *The Call,* United States

"Every so often a book comes along that jolts us, commanding attention and inspiring the embrace of goodness, truth and beauty. Ryan Messmore has gifted us with such a book. The story of Ryan and Karin's love and marriage, told against the backdrops of Jewish betrothal practices and the Bible's account of God's covenant love for creation, is delightful and challenging. What kind of people will our sexual practices shape us to become? Ryan Messmore explores the question in this intimate and profound b~~~~ ~~~~~
-Rod Thompson, Former National Princ
New Zealand and Minister, Springwood
Australia

D1293225

"Our culture has become increasingly confused about marriage and its meaning, but Ryan Messmore has helped clarify the importance of this vital institution. By recounting his own courtship and engagement and illuminating the full, rich picture of marriage throughout the Old and New Testaments, we begin to gain a glimpse of marriage as God intended it. What's more, Ryan has given us greater insight into Christ's passionate pursuit of His bride." **–Jim Daly,** President, Focus on the Family, United States

"Ryan Messmore has a gift for sharing wisdom in a winsome and accessible way. This book is profound, well written and short—a trifecta! Messmore points out the false stories we tell ourselves today about love, sex and marriage, and proposes a more excellent way. *In Love* will help readers place their own lives and loves in the right story. I'll be sharing it with friends. So should you."
-Ryan T. Anderson, Ph.D., Senior Research Fellow, The Heritage Foundation, and author of *Truth Overruled: The Future of Marriage and Religious Freedom*, United States

"Ryan Messmore brings the ancient Jewish betrothal tradition to life in a way that helps us revitalize modern-day relationships and also understand the larger biblical story. From questioning phrases like 'fall in love' to exploring pre-engagement counselling to describing sex as body language, this book helps readers approach their own love stories with intentionality and hope."
-Kelly Monroe Kullberg, Founder, The Veritas Forum and author of *Finding God Beyond Harvard*, United States

"In this economic yet comprehensive and elegant work, Dr Ryan Messmore guides his readers into a relational world, rich with hope and meaning. Drawing on his courtship, engagement and marriage to Karin, Ryan shows us that among other things love is an action. Referencing Jewish betrothal practices and Holy Scripture, Ryan places sexual desire and intercourse in a newer and fuller context; one that hovers over the question, 'What kind of people will certain sexual practices shape us to become?' Dr Messmore has written a grounded, compelling, richly-textured book that is wise and practical. The personal or confessional nature of *In Love* makes it very good reading."

-Paul Henderson, author of *Athanasius: someone from nothing* and *No Ordinary People: exploring what it means to be human*, Australia

"To anyone thoroughly catechized in the sexual revolution, this book and the story it tells will seem bizarre. But anyone willing to listen to the story and the carefully crafted Big Picture of love and sexuality Ryan describes here will find a beauty and truth not available in the small vision on offer in Western culture today."

-John Stonestreet, President, the Chuck Colson Center for Christian Worldview, United States

"This book is a great read and delves into the depths of an authentic dating, engagement and wedding journey! In a personal and even vulnerable way, it illumines the deeper design of sex and marriage, and provides historical as well as practical insights for anyone desiring to be 'in love'. Our confused culture needs the higher vision that this story provides. I hope many young adults, especially, will read this book."

-Paul Ninnes, Co-founder and Director, Real Talk International, Australia

"*In Love* drew me into three beautifully woven love stories. The result is a vision for relationships that is exciting and achievable, and which reminds us of what we were made for. What makes it so compelling is that Ryan narrates—rather than merely argues for—that vision. I cannot wait to get this book into the hands of every young adult and deep thinker I know!"

-Greg Fleming, CEO, Parenting Place and Co-founder, Venn Foundation, New Zealand

In Love:
The Larger Story of
Sex and Marriage

Ryan Messmore

Modotti Press

Published in 2017 by Modotti Press (An Imprint of Connor Court Publishing).

Copyright © Ryan Messmore

Connor Court Publishing Pty Ltd.
PO Box 7257
Redland Bay QLD 4165
sales@connorcourt.com
www.connorcourt.com

Phone 0497 900 685

ISBN: 978-1-925501-38-4

Cover design, Ian James

Printed in Australia

To Miriam

"'Love! Do you know the meaning of the word?'
'How should I not?' said the Lady. 'I am in love. In love,
do you understand? Yes, now I love truly. ... I am in Love
Himself ...'" —*The Great Divorce*, C. S. Lewis

∞

During a typical betrothal in ancient Israel, a young man
offered a cup of wine to his bride to seal their covenant.
After the ceremony, they would depart from each other
and perhaps not see each other for another year while
he built a room for them onto his father's homestead.
When the room was ready, he returned to claim her as his
bride, consummate the marriage, and inaugurate a grand,
celebratory feast.

During the Last Supper, Jesus handed his disciples a
cup of wine. He then told them he would soon depart
to prepare rooms for them in his Father's house. He
also promised to return one day to claim the church as
his bride, inaugurating what Scripture describes as "the
wedding supper of the Lamb" (Revelation 19:9).

Contents

1

A TALE OF TWO STORIES

Our eyes met across a crowded chapel. Well, actually, my eye caught her blonde hair and radiant face; I don't think she noticed me at all.

It was a warm Friday evening during my first semester at Duke University in Durham, North Carolina. I was walking toward the door of a small chapel in which Duke's InterVarsity Christian Fellowship met each week. As the "greeter", she welcomed people at the start of the gathering and wished them well as they left. Or perhaps she was handing out some sort of flyer. I forget; all I recall is what she looked like. Her image took up instant and permanent residence in my memory.

Who was this angel wearing a black dress, and what was she doing at Duke? I should have asked her name, but as I approached the door my nerves took over. I could barely talk. "Don't trip", I thought to myself. "Don't stare, but don't look away, but don't look obvious. Don't walk too fast, but don't look like a slacker either."

Finally I arrived at the door, took the flyer from her, and perhaps managed to utter, "bye". I asked someone her name and then headed back to my dorm to consult the facebook. Not "The Facebook" (it was 1993—a decade before Mark Zuckerberg launched that) but the book the university published with pics of the freshman class.* I found her: Karin Stoskopf, from Salina, Kansas. She was beautiful. I was smitten.

It was love at first sight.

Breaking the Ice

I managed to avoid talking to Karin the rest of the year. I desperately wanted to get to know her, but I thought she was in a different league. Thus, I admired her from afar.

At the beginning of our second year in college, one of my sisters, with whom I am a triplet, came to visit me. Upon arriving on campus one Friday afternoon, I took Tara to an InterVarsity meeting. We walked in late to a very crowded room and within a second my heart stopped. I scanned only two empty seats and they were right next to HER. Tara sat down beside Karin; I took the next seat over. Then, the InterVarsity leader announced an icebreaker exercise: "Find someone you don't know and spend the next five to ten minutes getting acquainted with them". Without flinching, my sister turned and started talking to Karin, oblivious to my feelings for her. I'd been gun-shy about approaching this blonde Kansas sunflower[1] for an entire year, but Tara had been on campus for 30 minutes and was talking up a storm with her!

My opportunity, though, would quickly come. Thanks to a

* Readers in both Australia and the United States will *recognise* differences in some of my words, spellings, and uses of grammar. My friends Down Under will hopefully forgive me for saying, "going to college" when referring to university (and for mentioning my "freshman" and "senior" year), "root beer" when describing sarsaparilla, and "mom" instead of "mum" (I tried it the other way, but just couldn't do it!). However, this book does use English/Australian rather than American spellings. Thus, I ask my friends and *neighbours* in the U.S. to *sympathise* in good *humour* with all the "-ise" and "-our" words, as well as my references to *counselling, jewellery, fulfil* and so forth. These are two countries separated by a common language!

wonderfully creative youth group leader I had growing up, I developed a special interest in *The Chronicles of Narnia*. Upon reading more of C. S. Lewis' books in college, I decided to create a course exploring the theology embedded in his children's stories. The university eventually approved it as a half-credit course. At first, though, I simply offered the sessions as informal opportunities to read and discuss the books with others. I passed around a sign-up sheet at an InterVarsity meeting to see if anyone was interested.

The result would change my life forever.

∞

Thus begins my love story with Karin, which anchors my reflections throughout the following chapters. I tell it *as a story* on purpose. In fact, a common desire for a better story grounded our initial relationship. In college, Karin and I both aspired for a compelling alternative to the script underlying Duke's "hook-up" culture. We were disappointed with the shallowness of its romantic vision and the incoherence of its sexual ethic. We wanted to understand the terrain of dating and love in a more healthy, hopeful and perhaps even holy way—one that would guide us toward beauty and intimacy and draw us into something bigger than ourselves. This book tells how we discovered that larger, better story.

It's worth asking, though, why a story is the appropriate, and even necessary, form of this book. What makes narratives, such as the *Narnia* tales or a memoir, so powerful for conveying deep relational truth?

Why Stories?

Consider the following two episodes.

A few years ago, in the middle of my son's soccer game, he lost his shoe running toward the ball. As it went flying off his foot and through the air, I questioned my ability to teach my kids the basics of life. It was a very unfortunate event.

During an airplane flight the following weekend, a movie was shown in which a young woman lost her shoe running away from a ball. It was the stroke of midnight, and she didn't stop to pick it up. This proved to be a very fortunate incident, indeed!

The same event can take on very different meaning depending on the larger narrative in which it fits. Whether it's my son Christopher or Cinderella, we all live according to some story that helps make sense of our daily actions and decisions. We "tell stories because that is how we perceive, and indeed relate to, the world. What we see close up … we make sense of by drawing on story-forms already more or less known to us and placing the information within them".[2]

In other words, we all carry basic assumptions about reality that shape how we interpret our lives. These assumptions may be conscious or subconscious, but they are always at work providing meaning and purpose to characters and events. Story is "the best way of talking about the way the world actually is",[3] i.e., full of people pursuing goals but inevitably facing challenges in reaching them. This is especially the case when pursuing something as personal and challenging as sex and marriage.

When it comes to discussing these topics, we're tempted to jump in with very passionate arguments about freedom, equality, rights, interpersonal love, and so forth. We don't often take time, however, to evaluate the larger stories in which these terms operate. Many of us may not even be aware that our opinions and attitudes, the meaning of the terms we use, and even our actions are shaped by narratives that linger just below the surface of consciousness.

These are important issues. Perhaps no other factor has elicited more joy or led to more pain than assumptions about sex and marriage. If we want to understand them in a coherent way, we need to ask, "What is the larger story in which these ideas fit, and how does that story help to mould their meaning?" I want to suggest that part of the confused and incoherent direction that our society has taken on these topics is due to today's dominant cultural script. To switch metaphors, the cultural soundtrack playing in the background of our lives has influenced the way Christians and non-Christians hear and make sense of words like "love", "sex", and "marriage"; and this context shapes their understanding and expectations of engagements and weddings.

This book is about two love stories that generate different views of sex and marriage. One of those stories dominates in modern Western culture; the other is very different, having to do with the process of betrothal leading to marriage in ancient Israel.

The Dominant Story, Part 1: Erotic Play

The modern, dominant story was actually crystallised for me the year before I went to college. From my hometown of Marlton, New Jersey, I travelled to Washington, D.C. to take part in a week-long leadership development program. All participants were housed in a hotel and placed with roommates from other states. That week our hotel also hosted a national high school cheerleading convention. One evening my roommate—let's call him Mike—walked through the door smiling big and breathing heavy. He proceeded to boast, in detail, about what he had just done with a cheerleader whom he happened to encounter in the hotel stairwell.

Two things struck me about this: first, how quickly they must have accomplished their escapade (in order to avoid being interrupted by someone else using the stairs); second, how quickly they advanced from introducing themselves to reaching down each other's pants. At that moment I realised I wasn't only in a different city, I had stepped into a very different story. Compared to my friends and family, this Casanova had a different way of seeing things and a different sense of normal. Certain acts carried an alternative meaning for Mike than they did for me.

What sort of story provides that meaning? What underlying assumptions make sense of this approach?

I call it the "Erotic Play" Story. It's the story that Tom Wolfe narrates in colourful detail in his novel *I Am Charlotte Simmons*, which is set at a university closely resembling Duke.[4] It's the story that a Duke student captured in her mock senior thesis in "horizontal academics", in which she "researched" her sexual exploits with 13 student-athletes.[5] Beginning in my first year at college, I would see this story's influence across the campus, by walking on Friday night through a "kegger" party or on Saturday morning down a dorm hallway. (You never knew whom you might see leaving the room—or even still in the bed—of a hung-over dormmate.)

In this story, sex is viewed merely as erotic play between consenting adults. The plot line focuses on looking good and maximising pleasure. My D.C. roommate Mike is a protagonist of this narrative; he sidestepped any cultural taboos present in the early 1990s, avoided the shackles of any commitment, and overcame any possible awkwardness involved in reaching into another person's personal space. Mike seeks pure recreational fun—testosterone-releasing, ego-boosting, pleasure-indulging sport. For him, sex seems to bear no deeper meaning and serve no higher purpose. It's not an expression of love. It's not tied to marriage. It's simply erotic play.

The Dominant Story, Part 2: Intimate Connection

Although this sort of promiscuous attitude is celebrated in certain kinds of music and movies, many people claim that sex means something more: it communicates care between lovers who share an intimate bond. This view holds that "going all the way" with someone should be special and should emerge out of a deep emotional connection. It understands that having sex is a way of being known at one's deepest level.

In short, many today still assume that sex should be bound up with romantic love and even insist that this sort of love is a prerequisite for sleeping together. Most of my Christian friends resonate with this assumption. So, today's dominant story is not exhausted by the view of sex as merely erotic play but also has room for another view: what I call sex as *intimate connection*.

Peers in my freshman ethics class articulated this "Intimate Connection" Narrative quite explicitly. One day marriage and sexual ethics emerged as topics of discussion. When asked about the purpose of sex, most of the students asserted that it's a natural way to express and enhance intimacy. When asked about marriage, most defined it as a relationship in which you get to journey through life with your most intimate partner. As one prominent author and advocate would later define it, marriage is your relationship with your "Number One Person".[6] In other words, most of us assumed that the basis of marriage is personal intimacy. We all presupposed that, at its best, the purpose of sex is to express love—understood as a feeling—and marriage is a relationship with the person to whom one feels closest. One researcher refers to this as the "soul-mate model of marriage", emphasising emotional intensity and personal fulfilment.[7] As Chelsea Clinton would say years later, "I certainly believe that all of my friends should have the right, as Marc and I did, to marry their *best friend*".[8]

I didn't realise it at the time, but a theologian who worked in that very same building, just down the hall, would provide me four years later with some different moral categories with which to work. When I entered these same debates in graduate school, Stanley Hauerwas[9] got me asking, "How does sex serve a community's pursuit of the common good?" Moreover, an undergraduate class with philosopher Alasdair MacIntyre prompted me to raise additional questions like, "What kind of people will certain sexual practices shape us to become?"[10] Needless to say, most of us weren't asking those sorts of questions our first year in college.

Questioning the Dominant Story

Compared with the "Erotic Play" Narrative, the "Intimate Connection" Story seems morally preferable. During our time in college, though, Karin and I began to ask some questions about it: If the peers in my first-year ethics class eventually got married, they probably expected and demanded faithful monogamy from their spouse (and promised as much in their wedding vows). If they were pressed, we wondered what sort of rationale they could provide for such fidelity. If marriage is based on feelings of love, and if sex expresses those feelings, what happens when a husband or wife "falls in love" with someone else? In that case, what compelling reason does the dominant story provide for staying married?

I suspect that most of my Christian friends who believed that marriage is based on feelings of love also thought that couples should wait until marriage to have sex. But if sex is essentially a means of expressing trust and intimacy, why would two people who feel deeply for each other, and safe with each other, wait until marriage to express it? To the degree that "safe sex" removes the fear of pregnancy, what exactly grounds the moral judgment against sleeping with someone before marriage?

Both views of sex—i.e., that it's merely *erotic play* or the expression of an *intimate connection*—actually fit within the same larger story. Combining these two assumptions we can refer to it as modern culture's "EPIC" (short for "Erotic Play or Intimate Connection") Story. Within this narrative, what matters is the freedom for individuals to express themselves as they wish. What people do with their bodies and whom they choose to do it with is their own business, so long as both parties consent and nobody is harmed. You might say that this story is about the freedom to write one's own love story.

But neither the Erotic Play nor the Intimate Connection Story makes sense of what so many people long for and promise each other upon saying, "I do". The dominant EPIC Narrative cannot explain a marital commitment to unconditional love, exclusivity, permanence, and children.

Karin and I wanted a better story.

The Jewish Betrothal Story

Although we'd read famous romances like *Romeo and Juliet* and watched tear-jerker films like *Ghost*, the most compelling narrative turned up in a most unexpected place. We found it when we happened upon a description of the traditional Jewish betrothal process prevalent during biblical times.

Here's how that process would have worked for a typical Israelite groom (*Chatan* in Hebrew) and bride (*Kallah* in Hebrew), whom I will refer to simply as Chad and Kayla.[11]

Their eyes might have first met across a crowded well, a typical context for meeting a potential spouse in ancient Israel. Alternatively, perhaps Chad's father had already arranged their destiny with Kayla's father for political or financial reasons.

Whatever motivated the desire for matrimony, Chad and his father wrote out the marriage's terms and conditions on a covenant document (*ketubah*). They then travelled to Kayla's house, with one or two witnesses, to discuss these expectations with her father. If they agreed, Chad offered Kayla a cup of wine (representing the blood of an animal), saying something like, "this cup represents a covenant in blood". If she accepted the offer of marriage, she sipped from the cup. This act sealed the betrothal (*kiddushin*). Chad then said, "I am your husband, and you are my wife", and Kayla responded, "I am your wife, and you are my husband". Typically, Chad also presented his bride with a betrothal gift, either in the form of money or a ring made of precious metal.

Upon sealing the covenant, the bride and groom left each other and perhaps didn't see one another for an entire year! What was going on? Chad returned home and began building a room (*chuppah*) onto his father's homestead. This addition to the house, which could take up to a year to finish, would be the new residence for the bride and groom. During this time, if Kayla entered a market or other public place, she covered her face with a veil. This signalled to other men in town that she was already betrothed and prevented the groom from seeing her until their wedding night.

When the additional room was complete, Chad gathered his family and friends and set off to claim his bride. On that day, Kayla's mother and bridesmaids helped her in a ritual bath (*mikveh*) that symbolised spiritual cleansing. Then they anointed her with perfumed oils, helped her into her wedding garments, and adorned her with jewels.[12] Not knowing the precise hour her groom would come, Kayla and her companions waited expectantly throughout the day and possibly into the night.

Typically, the best friend ran ahead and announced Chad's arrival by blowing a ram's horn (*shofar*). The couple then processed back to their new home. Israelites held this wedding procession in the highest regard. The bride and groom wore crowns[13] and were called "king" and "queen" for the day.

Upon reaching the house of Chad's father, the couple listened to the covenant document read aloud, repeated their solemn declaration ("I am your husband ..." and "I am your wife ..."), received a blessing, and again sipped from a cup of wine. Then, in their *chuppah* room, they consummated their marriage covenant sexually. Chad's friend guarded the door and announced to the crowd when the consummation had taken place. As custom dictated, the newlyweds spent seven continuous days inside this bridechamber. During these seven days, the two families celebrated together and, when Chad and Kayla emerged from the bridechamber, held a final wedding supper.[14]

Framing Our Story

I refer to this as the "Jewish Betrothal Story" or "Covenant Love Story". Obviously, compared with the story that guided my D.C. roommate and the peers in my college ethics class, this ancient Jewish account reveals an alternative set of attitudes and practices. Sex, love, and marriage assume different meanings and play different roles within these narratives.

In the EPIC Story, love is a feeling and marriage is based on that sort of love; sex is an erotic activity that either satisfies an appetite or expresses an emotion, and it isn't necessarily tied to marriage or having children. In the Jewish Betrothal Story, the centre of gravity isn't erotic pleasure, or even emotional intimacy; instead, it's the uniting of two people in a committed, life-long, family-expanding bond. As it operates within this narrative, love isn't as much a feeling as an act of the will, and marriage is based not on the emotion of love but instead on covenant faithfulness. Sex, in turn, gains its deepest meaning as the act that consummates and renews that covenant. One of the reasons that marriage has covenantal permanence and is consummated by sex is because of its inherent orientation toward children.

The following pages recount how Karin and I came not just to *understand* (mentally) but also to *enter into* and *participate* in this alternative narrative.

To be sure, we didn't wish to adopt this particular Jewish process in its entirety. Compared to the tradition of arranged marriages, we were thankful that we had a large say in choosing to enter our relationship. We also prize the freedom and equality that women generally enjoy in the West today compared to women in biblical times, and we disagree with the institution of polygamy, not to mention the practice of keeping mistresses. In short, there's a lot about the cultural, social, and political context of ancient Israel that is problematic from our modern Western perspective.

Why, then, look back to it for relationship guidelines? After all, there are lots of cultural traditions surrounding marriage; why pay attention to this particular one? The simple answer is that the Jewish Betrothal Story illumines the greatest love story ever told: God's relationship with us. (I'll refer to this as the "Grand Love Story".) What attracted us to this cultural script are the scriptural cues it unlocks. The more parallels we discovered between Chad and Kayla's story and the Grand Love Story of all of history, the more intrigued we became.

Karin and I identified four stages of the ancient Jewish process that could provide a framework for our relationship: 1) desiring marriage, 2) entering a covenant, 3) preparing for its fulfilment, and 4) consummating it sexually.

For my relationship with Karin, following these stages yielded significant results. The Jewish Betrothal Story changed the way we talked (we gave up using phrases like "fall in love" and "love at first sight"). It changed the way we approached our engagement (in college we fasted once a week for our relationship and went through *pre-engagement* counselling). It changed the way we approached issues of sex (we began rethinking contraception) and it deepened our view of marriage. Most importantly, it broadened our understanding and appreciation of the biblical story and of God's relationship with His people.

Simply put, the world of romantic love and sexual ethics looks different when seen through the lens of this narrative. *In Love* describes our attempt to live out this ancient story's wisdom on a modern university campus.

This Story's Outline

Chapter 2 narrates how we began dating and then frames the way we came to think—and speak—about love. The four subsequent chapters follow the four broad stages of the ancient Jewish betrothal process: desiring intimate, bodily communion (Chapter 3 on physical relationships), entering the process of covenant making (Chapter 4 on engagement), preparing for its faithful fulfilment (Chapter 5 on getting ready for marriage), and celebrating its consummation

(Chapter 6 on sex). Chapter 7 reaches beyond earthly marriages and reveals the larger, more ancient love story in which our relationships participate: the biblical story of God's marital union with His people. This is the eternal union of dwelling "in Love" Himself.

In short, this book is a narrative of how our lives and love story became swept up into an ancient, beautiful story much larger than ourselves. It's a story of grace, for we didn't undertake this journey perfectly, and I'm sure we haven't understood it fully. I suspect we've only scratched the surface. But it's a story that has given us purpose and direction, and we share it in the hope that it might provide encouragement and assistance to others.

2

WHAT IS LOVE?

At the beginning of my second year in college, I passed around a sign-up sheet to see if any InterVarsity members were interested in taking my *Chronicles of Narnia* course. Later that evening when I looked at the sheet, my eyes fixed upon one name in particular. The signature was bigger and more elegant than the others, and to me the cursive letters were penned with perfect shape and slant: "Karin Stoskopf".

Suddenly both fear and excitement stirred within me. I was excited because, finally, after a year of wondering, I had written evidence that Karin knew I existed. More than that, she was interested in something I was doing; she voluntarily committed her time to take my course.

During that semester, I poured myself into teaching *Narnia*. When discussing the seven stories in class, we ate food that the characters ate in the particular book assigned for that week. We also met somewhere on campus that resembled a setting in the book. For *Prince Caspian*, which contains the scene of Caspian's nurse taking him to the top of the castle tower in the dark of night, we met on top of the Duke Chapel tower after sundown. For *The Silver Chair* we even journeyed to Sweetwater, Tennessee, home of America's largest underground lake, where our class slept overnight in a cave.

I wanted these discussions to be special. My goal was that each student would share in the magic of Narnia and come to know better the Great Lion himself. I wanted them to care as much as I did and to track with me as I led them through the tales. Karin did that superbly. One of her wonderful traits is listening—not just sitting quietly and allowing others to talk, but actively listening. During the *Narnia* sessions she conveyed her interest through facial expressions and well-timed "uh-huhs". What I especially treasured was her head tilt. She would cock her head slightly to the left like those awkward poses you have to strike when sitting for a formal portrait. Those couple degrees of neck alignment shouted to me the calls of a boisterous charismatic congregation: "preach it ... that's right ... keep going ... Amen!" It was the affirmation I needed, and it came from the most warm, glowing, and delicate face this side of Cair Paravel.

First Date

Throughout the semester I held to a personal promise not to flirt with or even linger after class talking to Karin. I didn't want ulterior motives to shape my approach to teaching the course. The day after the semester ended, though, I bumped into her in the Bryan Student Center. Without any prior small talk (I feared that if I allowed any time to pass, I'd back out), I asked, "Would you like to have dinner?"

She smiled and said, "Yes".

Again, excitement and fear!

We set the time and place and then I went to study for my final exams ... and to begin fasting. I had offered to take her to the nicest— read *most expensive*—restaurant on campus. With my two sisters and me in college at the same time, I was on the least expensive dining plan, so I stopped eating at that moment to save enough "meal points" to cover both Karin and me at The Oak Room.

It was worth it. I'm sure the food was good, but all I remember was how delicious our time together was. The conversation flowed almost too smoothly, and it seemed like we were the only ones in the room. I didn't want it to end.

She was beautiful. I was smitten.

I had fallen in love.

Or had I?

On Not Falling in Love

During this period we started to learn more about the nature of ancient Jewish love stories. The first stage of that narrative was one of desire for a relationship. What sort of desire might there have been at that stage? Putting myself in Chad and Kayla's shoes, who represent the typical Jewish husband (*Chatan*) and wife (*Kallah*) during biblical times, I imagine there was a hope and desire to grow in intimacy, trust, affection, and, of course, physical attraction. But none of these feelings may have been present the first time the two saw each other. Given that their parents might have arranged the relationship, the betrothal ceremony could have been the first time Chad and Kayla even met. In the ancient Jewish context, there were likely other factors motivating the desire for marriage, including social status, economic security, physical protection, a good reputation through offspring, and so forth.

Whatever feeling animated their decision, I would not call it romantic love, at least not the sort that motivates relationships today. In that older context, rather than an emotion that is experienced beforehand, love seemed to be something that one committed to work toward in the future. In other words, this isn't a story in which "*first* comes love, *then* comes marriage". Rather, love seemed to be something that was learned *as a result* of enduring the ups and downs of married life.[15]

That struck me as a very different meaning of the word "love".

Our modern use of the term seems rather loose and flexible in comparison. After all, I employed this same word "love" to describe my feelings for my mom, my country, my penguin tie, and now my new romantic interest, Karin (although it would take another year or two before I dared utter that word to her). I also casually expressed "love" for watching Duke basketball, eating Alaskan king crab legs, listening to the soundtrack from *The Mission*, playing soccer, and quoting lines from *A Few Good Men*. And yet this was also the same word that I used in reference to God.

That was the clue that, somewhere along the line, my reliance on the term had run amok. According to 1 John 4:8, love is the very nature of God; it is also the new command that Jesus gave his disciples at the Last Supper. Could the love that Jesus calls for, which he expressed through his own agony and death on the cross, really be the same thing I felt upon watching a Jack Nicholson courtroom scene? Was it the same thing that I felt toward Karin?

As I contemplated this word's meaning, I discovered a fascinating claim about 1 Corinthians 13, commonly known as "the love chapter" of Scripture. There the Apostle Paul uses fifteen different words to describe love (*agape* in Greek), some of which are typically translated into English as (predicate) adjectives. "Love is patient, love is kind. ... it is not proud ... it is not self-seeking ..." (verses 4-5). In the original Greek, however, each of these words is a *verb*.[16]

Think about that for a moment. To communicate what love is, Paul uses verbs. This suggests that love is active and dynamic and moving. It is something we *do*, not merely something we *feel*. It is a commitment we forge with our will, not just a stirring we sense in our heart. Love is an action, not just an attraction.

The Act of Love

What kind of action does love name?

I found some pretty direct guidance in the Gospel of John. For example, during the Last Supper Jesus says to his disciples, "A new command I give you: Love one another. As I have loved you, so you must love one another" (John 13:34). All three instances of the word "love" in this verse are the Greek verb *agapao*. The phrase "as I have loved you" referred to Jesus' act of washing his disciples feet—their filthy, grimy, smelly, calloused feet. This was servant's work, not the typical act of an esteemed teacher, let alone a king. Jesus, though, took on this role as a humble act of love.

So love is a verb that has to do with serving or promoting the good of another.

I read further in John's gospel. In Chapter 15 Jesus repeats his command and then offers an additional explanation: "My command is this: Love each other as I have loved you. Greater love has no one than this: to lay down one's life for one's friends" (John 15:12-13). According to Jesus, love is also an act of giving oneself for another. Somebody who loves doesn't turn in on herself but gives herself away; she offers herself as a gift to the other. God so loved the world that He gave His only son (John 3:16), and that son would demonstrate this self-giving to its fullest extent on the cross. "This is how we know what love is: Jesus Christ laid down his life for us. And we ought to lay down our lives for our brothers and sisters. ... Dear children, let us not love with words or speech but with actions and in truth" (1 John 3:16-18).

Scripture, of course, provides more than a couple of verses

about love. In a sense, the entire biblical story testifies to what it's all about. The Christian story is a love story. It's the story about a God who we might say goes outside of Himself to work for the good of creation and to give his life for the sake of a covenant union with His people.

Created in the Image of Love

Understanding love as this kind of a verb was one of the most consequential concepts I wrestled with in college. This insight goes to the heart of some of the deepest truths of life, including who God is and what it means to be human.

Love (*agape*, meaning unconditional, sacrificial love) is identified in 1 John 4:8, 16 as the very nature of God. Just try to get your head around that! (I spent the next 12 years making that attempt and eventually wrote my doctoral dissertation at Oxford on the Trinity—a doctrine that I believe is required by the claim that God is love.) The Christian deity is a threefold communion in which the Father and Son eternally give themselves to each other, empowered by the Holy Spirit. This means that the inner nature of God is active—a dynamic fellowship of self-sharing in which three are united in one.

In addition to how we understand God, the definition of love also shapes our concept of what it means to be a human person. We are made in the image of a God whose nature is love; therefore, as human beings, we are in our deepest nature *lovers*. That is, we are relational beings able and called to give ourselves for the good of others.[17] "I" only has meaning in the context of relationship, as who I am is largely bound up with whom or what I relate to.[18] The purpose and goal of life is a communion—a fellowship of sharing that unites people with God, others, and the rest of creation. This is who we are and for what we were made.

Think about someone whom you consider to excel in being human—that is, a good person—perhaps someone like Mother Teresa. What is it that distinguishes someone like Mother Teresa from someone like my D.C. roommate Mike? Does it not include the way they relate to others—more precisely, their commitment to offer their self in pursuit of others' goods versus their use of others for their own good? Outward-focused, self-giving love is the end and the perfection of what it means to be human.

Speaking of Love

Understanding love as self-donation also made more sense of the Jewish Betrothal Story. In that context, what the spouses committed to was not *felt* love but *active* love, not *emotions* but *actions*—the actions specified in the covenant.

This seemed to me to provide a much more reliable basis for a relationship. Although Chad and Kayla likely hoped to fan the flame of passion in their marriage, the flame's absence was not sufficient grounds for dissolving it. Even as the mutual feelings that a couple did develop waxed and waned over time (as is typical in long-term relationships), the expectations and responsibilities of self-giving love did not change.

I began an experiment to use the word "love" as often as possible as a verb. That meant giving up some common phrases in which love, especially in its romantic sense, is used as a noun. Gone from my vocabulary was not only "fall in love" but also "love at first sight". Just like a young man seeing his soon-to-be-wife for the first time at their betrothal, love wasn't truly possible the moment I first saw Karin. I hadn't yet done anything for her, given anything to her, or committed to seek her good.

Nor had I "fallen in love" with her. The more I thought about that phrase, the more it reminded me of an old TV commercial in which an elderly lady shrieks, "I've fallen, and I can't get up". Not a romantic image! Self-sacrificing love isn't a ditch or a sinkhole that we accidently fall into. Nor is it something we can fall out of, like a tree house or a top bunk.

When we speak about "falling in love", we're really referring to the intensity of our feelings toward someone. It's true that romantic feelings often seem to sneak up on us and render us helpless, as happened the first time I saw Karin. It's also true that these feelings are natural and healthy and that they serve a good purpose (see Chapter 3). But these sudden, debilitating, and often unpredictable feelings aren't love (and they don't make a reliable basis for marriage). Why not call them what they are?

I now say that when I first set eyes on Karin, it was "infatuation at first sight". There might be a better term, but this alternative communicates the truth of what I felt and even suggests why I felt it. I was infatuated with a girl I thought was hot. The action and commitment of love hadn't yet entered the picture. I fell for her because her beauty was arresting, and I'm wired to respond to beauty.

Our Song

Sure enough, as we spent more time together over the following semester, we experienced feelings of not only attraction but also annoyance. The frustrations began when Karin didn't respond to any of my written notes. I left short poems on the whiteboard mounted on her dorm room door. Then I waited ... and waited ... and waited. Nothin'.

Eventually, I figured out that I'd left these romantic odes on the wrong door! Another "Karen" lived down the hall from the one I was pursuing. It was slightly awkward when this stranger opened the door and found me, pen in hand, waxing romantic on her board.

When I finally located the correct room, I entered only to find another guy sitting on Karin's bed. As I later learned, Karin was helping him study for a calculus test, but at that moment I read it the wrong way. Hurt and dejected, I walked off. I fell out of infatuation about as quickly as I had fallen in.

When I reached the sidewalk outside her dorm, Karin leaned out her first-floor window and called to me. Reluctantly, I walked over to her. She could tell that I was upset, and I could sense that she was nervous. She placed a small, portable stereo on the window ledge and stammered, "I need to go to the bathroom, but I want you to hear this". In a surreal moment, I listened by myself to a cheesy country song by Boy Howdy called "If I Were You I'd Fall in Love with Me". It wasn't the most sophisticated ballad, but her willingness to play it did what was needed for our relationship at that point. My feelings were back, and I desired to keep pursuing her.

As I walked to my dorm that evening, I thought about the irony of what had just transpired: "I think we now have something to call 'our song' ... and it has the phrase 'fall in love' in its title". Unbelievable!

3

STAGE 1: DESIRING BODILY COMMUNION
Physical Relationships

The first stage of the Jewish Betrothal Story entails a young man like Chad wanting to unite with a young woman like Kayla. I was at that same stage with Karin.

I noted in Chapter 1 that, as a typical Jewish couple during biblical times, Chad and Kayla may have met at a well. "[A]t the time of Jesus, if you were an eligible young Jewish man looking for an eligible young Jewish woman, you would not go to a bar or to a club. Instead, you would go where the ladies were to be found: the local well."[19] Moses met his future wife, Zipporah, at a well (Exodus 2:15-17, 21), as did Jacob with his future bride Rachel (Genesis 29:1-11). Isaac's wife, Rebekah, was also identified at a well, but not by Isaac himself. His father Abraham sent a servant to find Isaac a bride; Isaac didn't have much say in the matter (Genesis 24:11-19).

Isaac's story reveals one of the many differences between Chad and Kayla's culture and ours: Karin and I were free to pursue someone with whom we were infatuated; Chad and Kayla's decision was controlled to a much greater extent by their fathers. Our modern-day search for a significant other often leads to assessing a potential spouse in terms of Mr. or Ms. Right; Chad and Kayla, in contrast, would not likely enter marriage with these sorts of (impossible) expectations. (By the way, "Hauerwas' Law" states: *you always marry the wrong person!*[20] In other words, there's no Mr. or Ms. Right out there with whom, if you could only find them, you would be guaranteed a happy marriage.) Another cultural difference is that Karin and I had a lot of time to get to know each other before making the decision to marry; Chad and Kayla may not have known each other at all prior to getting betrothed. Moreover, Karin and I lived in the midst of a hook-up culture in which sex isn't necessarily linked to marriage and procreation; these were held much closer together in Chad and Kayla's society.

Despite the dissonance between our contexts, there's something Karin and I share in common with ancient Jewish couples like Chad and Kayla and young people across the planet throughout history: bodies charged with hormones, impulses, and desires. Given that they would perhaps not see each other for up to a year after their betrothal, Chad and Kayla had to cultivate the ability to wait for sex; if their romantic attraction was strong, that would have posed a challenge. Here Karin and I could relate very well!

Love Is Bodily

This first stage of our romantic relationship—the one I call "desiring intimate, bodily communion"—was thrilling. The months that Karin and I spent getting to know each other were some of the best we can remember. Perhaps you've been in that situation with another person where you can't stop thinking of each other, you always want to be together, and you can talk—or just stare into each other's eyes—for hours. And, of course, as the intimacy deepens, so too does the desire to (shall we say) commune bodily.

I sure felt this way for Karin; I didn't view sex merely as erotic play, but I found myself wanting to continue deepening our personal relationship through physical means. This shouldn't surprise us, for humans are inescapably physical beings. We are not essentially spirits who inhabit material bodies as neutral containers. Our personal unity is deeper than that. We don't just *have* bodies—in a real sense we *are* our bodies.

My body is integral to who I am as a relational person. What makes me uniquely me has a lot to do with my relationships with everything outside of me—my relationships with people (my wife, kids, extended family, friends, co-workers), objects (my favourite foods, clothes, books, music, television programs, car), and, I would emphasise, my Creator (who knows me by name and calls me according to His purposes).[21] Each of the persons and things named above represents one end of a relationship. What can be found on the other end? My body. That is, my body is the common location—the nexus—of all the relationships that make me uniquely me. The point is that, even though I am a relational being who cannot be reduced to physical matter, if you wanted to find me, you would look for my material body. As human persons, we experience the world and ourselves in a bodily way.

If that's true, and if love (the sacrificial *agape* kind) entails giving myself away for another, then love naturally entails my physical body. This doesn't mean only having sexual intercourse; there are numerous ways we give ourselves physically for the good of others. In fact, the more I thought about it, it seems like most ways of loving our neighbour involve us doing something bodily.

The Material vs. The Personal?

This was a new appreciation for me, for growing up in an evangelical church I tended to pit "personal relationship" over against "the material". I was led to believe that material things usually distract from or work against what really counts in a relationship: the emotional or spiritual connection.

But when I began to take inventory of my deepest personal relationships—with my family and friends, for example—I had to admit that they were mediated through material things. Helping someone study for an exam, giving them a ride home, taking flowers to them in the hospital, or even just sharing a chocolate bar—all of these ways of showing love involve physical objects or actions. After all, Jesus didn't command his disciples to *think fondly* about the thirsty, naked and imprisoned, but to bodily serve them with water, clothes, and physical presence.[22]

This was true of my relationship with Karin as well. When I abandoned the strategy of leaving poems on her whiteboard, I switched to writing her notes on paper or a keyboard (material objects). We also spent countless hours walking around the perimeter of the campus, as well as playing tennis, cheering at soccer games, and ballroom dancing together. These were all physical activities that fostered rather than distracted from personal intimacy with Karin.

On another occasion my emotions for Karin prompted me to give her a surprise gift. She let me know that she had given up ice cream for Lent, and the impending battle with her will power would be fierce. Therefore, one day as she walked from class to the parking lot, I left a pint-size container of Ben & Jerry's for her to find on the front hood of her car. Flirtation often disguises itself in wicked teasing. However, because I intended this gift as a symbol of affection, I had eaten all the ice cream (sometimes love requires sacrifices!) and filled the carton, instead, with her favourite chocolates.

The point is that personal relationship is mediated through, not opposed to, the physical and material.[23] We give ourselves to others—that is, we love—*with* and *through* and *as* our bodies.

The Deeper Design of Sexuality

In the early stages of a relationship, though, the desires to play tennis and share chocolates aren't the ones that scream the loudest. How should we think about the romantic impulses that reside at a more primal level? Are they simply the cravings of a natural appetite to be casually satisfied, or do they point to something deeper?

My D.C. roommate Mike took these impulses at face value; they weren't signals of anything more profound (like *agape*—i.e., self-giving love); they were simply physical urges to be satisfied with a willing partner. The dictates of *Eros* (the Greek god of love in its romantic or erotic sense) are to be obeyed as the final authority; they need no further justification.

Sexual cravings appear differently, though, if we were created for the purpose of communion. Our physical desires are aimed at something more profound; they are our natural wiring for loving, personal union. *Eros* is meant to serve *agape*, if we only had eyes to see it.

When my family goes to the beach, we sometimes spot a dolphin swimming in the ocean. Someone spots a fin breaking the surface of the water and alerts everyone else: "Look, there's a dolphin!" It's rare that we ever see anything more than the small, triangular fin; we usually don't see the whole animal. But we know they go together, so when you see the fin you picture the entire dolphin swimming just below the water line. An alien from another planet who has never seen a dolphin, however, would likely interpret things differently. If you said to the alien, "Look, there's a dolphin", the alien might associate "dolphin" simply with the small, visible triangle and wonder why you're so excited.

In a culture bent toward instant self-gratification, we've become aliens who are blind to the larger meaning of our sexuality. Our sexual desires abide very much above the surface of our consciousness; we are very aware of the reactions we experience when talking to a cute girl at a party or even walking by an attractive stranger on the street. We fail to see, though, that these reactions are connected to a deeper purpose that swims just below the surface. We place all our attention on what's immediately sensible, without picturing the larger good. We see body parts, but not the underlying person.

Simply put, the larger good is whole-person communion. What was true of Adam is true for all of us: we were not created to be alone.[24] We were meant for relationship, and we were given bodies, in part, as a means of relating.

Going even further, we were given *different* bodies, in part, as a means of relating in a certain way. The triune God of love, who is three persons in one godhead—unity in diversity—created human beings in His image as male and female (Genesis 1:27). That is, by creating us with a fundamental dimension of otherness, He enabled our sexuality to be a means of uniting. Anthony Esolen notes that the English word "sex" comes from the Latin *sexus*, meaning "divide".[25] We have a sex—maleness and femaleness—inscribed in our individual bodies. It is precisely this biological difference that enables us to make love, that is, to comprehensively unite across the male-female divide.[26]

"One-Flesh" Unions

In Jewish communities during biblical times, young men like Chad would have heard about this kind of bodily unity in the book of Genesis. As a text that he would have likely memorised as a boy,

Chad would be familiar with the claim that a man and his wife "become one flesh" (Genesis 2:24).

I had often heard this phrase, but I had not developed a deep understanding of what a one-flesh union is. Growing up I assumed that "one-flesh union" is a metaphor referring to a very intimate relationship. But I came to discover that this term can be more than just figurative language; it actually describes a reality that occurs when a husband and wife make love.

As Aristotle taught, different organs form one body when they work together to achieve one or more of that body's biological functions. In *Parts of Animals*, for example, he describes how the windpipe, larynx and lungs coordinate to achieve respiration.[27] They work together to accomplish a common biological end for the good of a single individual.

Among the bodily functions that Aristotle mentions are locomotion, digestion, sleeping and reproduction. You can think of many more. All but one of these functions can be achieved by the organs of a single body. The agent in digestion, for example, is an individual. Reproduction, however, cannot be achieved by oneself; it requires a male and female acting as a single unit, coordinated toward a single end. The agent in reproduction is not an individual but a couple. In the act of making love, they form a one-flesh union.

Thus, when we experience sexual urges, this is the deeper meaning to which they point: union with another. Romantic impulses are natural and healthy, but they are connected to a larger good: the full union of two entire persons, which we call marriage.

In other words, marriage is much more than a romantic bond based in emotional intimacy. What if it's a union not only of hearts and minds but also of bodies to form a one-flesh union? That would mean that relationships in which one-flesh unions aren't physically or biologically possible don't fit the definition of marriage. Two people may experience a deep emotional connection that inspires them to make sacrifices for and a long-term commitment to each other. But this sort of felt love isn't the essence of marriage; it can characterise deep friendships as well. Marriage differs from mere friendship in that spouses unite in the kind of way that performs a single bodily function, one that neither of their bodies could achieve on its own. Only in this sort of one-flesh union, oriented toward reproduction, do two persons give themselves bodily in the way that makes love across the sexual divide.

Promptings Toward Personal Communion

Thus, when we react physically in the presence of an attractive guy or girl, if we can see not just a body part but a person, we have a clue about that impulse's deeper purpose. If persons are meant to give themselves in love, we can see our physical reaction as a *prompting toward personal communion*. That is, we can interpret our sexual urges as the bodily expression of a deeper design—or the longing for a larger good—that swims below the surface of our consciousness. It's our design as potential partners in a one-flesh union; it's our longing for life together with another person.

In light of the communion for which we were made as human beings, it makes sense that our bodies naturally encourage that end. It was my bodily, hormonal reaction to Karin's physical appearance that prompted me to want to get to know her better, so that I could make the decision to act for her good—i.e., to love her.

Mistaking Physical Pleasure for Home

The problem is that these natural and healthy urges become so easily distorted. Whereas sexual desires are meant to be a catalyst or aid, we tend to make them the primary end. C. S. Lewis makes this point well. In talking about the enjoyment of certain pleasures, he says, "Our Father refreshes us on the journey with some pleasant inns, but will not encourage us to mistake them for home".[28] When we mistake the hotel for home, we end up using the body of the other as a means of self-gratification, rather than using our bodies as a means of self-gift.

With this temptation in mind, many of my Christian friends thought that, while physical touch should be neither completely indulged[29] nor completely suppressed,[30] there is a physical limit beyond which dating couples shouldn't go. Not surprisingly, one of the biggest topics of interest in my campus fellowship was what exactly that limit is—i.e., how far is too far physically for a couple before marriage.

The Magic Line

I referred to this question as the search for the "magic line", the line up to which a couple's physical relationship could go without sinning. Some of us weren't satisfied with this approach.

On a theoretical level, it seems to presume the existence of some random act that's the same for everyone, regardless of their character or self-control. And this act is discussed as if it floats around in the moral universe all by itself, simply as a principle disconnected from any larger context or story. The trick is simply to identify what it is. My philosophy professor Alasdair MacIntyre helped me to see that this approach to ethics isn't adequate. In *After Virtue* he wrote, "I can only answer the question 'What am I to do?' if I can answer the prior question 'Of what story or stories do I find myself a part?'"[31] The magic line approach addresses the former but ignores the latter.

On a practical level, discussions in college about "how far is too far" didn't focus much on how couples approach and engage all the acts that lay on the "safe side" of the line (whatever that is). As long as they avoid crossing the line, it doesn't seem to matter how quickly and in what order they do everything else. Holding hands, hugging, walking with an arm around his waist, running fingers through her hair, kissing on various levels—it seems that these become almost throw-away acts in which couples casually engage on the first few dates. I wondered if these gestures should carry more weight than that.

Also, the "magic line" approach seems to set a lot of us up to fail. By making everything before that point okay for anyone at any time, the freedom to walk right up to it is often too enticing. The only resource that most young people take with them into the back seat of a car is their prior mental commitment to a line. Nine times out of ten that's not enough! Without training one's desires ahead of time, the magic line approach too easily leads to the very thing it's supposed to help prevent: going too far.

In the end, it seems as if the "nothing until marriage" approach as well as the "up to the magic line" approach both suffer from the same problem. Neither seems to place intentional focus on the main issue: learning to discipline and order our desires so that we can act on them in a healthy way.

The Goal: Character

Rather than indulging or suppressing all impulses, or worrying only about those past a particular point, there's a different option: focusing on becoming the *kind of people* who can say yes to the right urges at the right time.

I believe a similar principle applies when thinking about money. In and of itself, money isn't bad, but it does have the power to tempt us with unhealthy attachment (i.e., greed). To those who place too much trust in wealth, Jesus says to give it all away.[32] One can't serve two masters at once.[33] The goal is to become the *kind of person* who can handle having a lot of money without succumbing to its temptation—that is, someone who can use it for good.

Likewise, romantic desires aren't bad, but they are easily perverted. If we cannot control them, we should not act on them. But the larger aim shouldn't be merely the avoidance of getting carried away; it should be the positive goal of developing a character that can respond to natural urges to promote healthy relationships.

To achieve this goal on a modern university campus, Karin and I needed to be intentional about developing one habit in particular: *self-control*. This was the key to being able to engage in a physical relationship without going too far and to walk through each stage slowly without going too fast. I knew I needed to take this seriously because I had already gone further than I would have liked with other girls. Thankfully, I hadn't gone "all the way", but I did know what it felt like to go beyond my own boundaries. If it was to be different with Karin, I knew I needed to cultivate better self-discipline.

Self-Control Takes Practice

But how does someone do that? By practicing saying "no" in other areas of life.

Again, thanks to MacIntyre's ethics class, during the time I was pursuing Karin I was also reading Aristotle's account of the virtues. Aristotle believed that people acquire self-control in a similar way to learning to play a sport or an instrument: through practice. By doing the same things over and over, these skills become habits. Habits, in turn, produce character. To make self-control a habit, Karin and I decided to find areas in our lives where we could practice saying no to various desires. We resolved to start small and build up our discipline.[34]

For Karin and me, that meant fasting. Before we started even holding hands, we fasted every Thursday. (I remember it clearly, for somehow it ALWAYS happened that Thursday was the day when some campus organisation offered free wine and cheese or my favourite meal went on a one-day sale at a campus eatery!) We did this not only to set aside time to pray for our relationship but also simply to train ourselves to tame our natural bodily urges.

I also looked for other ways to practice self-discipline. I tithed what little money I made from my part-time job, saying no to my desire to spend it on things I wanted (which often was more food). I observed the Sabbath, saying no to my desire to study for Monday's tests, even during final exam week. And I disciplined my tongue, saying no to my desire to tell Karin those three most powerful words: "I love you".

I realised that I can't separate my ability to love Karin physically from the way I live the rest of my life. After all, it is my same body engaged in all those activities (eating, spending money, studying). How could I mindlessly, repeatedly cater to its urges everywhere else and then suddenly expect to control them when I was with Karin, especially when those Karin-directed urges were the strongest?

Along with fasting, tithing, and observing the Sabbath, I decided to take a deliberate "wait until it hurts ... and then some" approach to touching Karin. I wouldn't ignore that aspect of our relationship, but I would handle it with great care. And so, as we got to know each other, we waited to hold hands.

We waited and waited and waited.

Looking back, I think this had positive effects for our relationship. Taking our time helped us to focus on communicating and getting to know each other, which was actually a lot of fun. But when we finally held hands for the first time—WOW! It was incredible. I remember it very vividly; the moment occurred while we sat on a grassy slope overlooking a pond in the campus gardens. Because we had taken this step so seriously, it was loaded with meaning. And like a good root beer, it had a sort of lingering effect on us. I couldn't believe it, but I didn't feel the need to rush ahead to the next level of physical touch. I wanted to dwell in that stage for a while. We simply held hands for weeks and weeks.

It may seem counterintuitive, but I think these disciplines and self-imposed boundaries helped to equip us with true freedom. Rather than being dominated by uncontrollable urges or external rules, we were free—i.e., we had the ability—to pursue a healthy physical relationship.

Eventually, we did walk slowly through further stages of physical intimacy like hugging and running fingers through each other's hair. (Guys, don't underestimate the intimacy of this act!) All this led up to the night at Myrtle Beach.

First Kiss

Dukies loved going to Myrtle after their final exams. Karin and I were only days away from saying goodbye to our second year in college. This farewell would be especially difficult, though, for we were both studying abroad the following academic year—me during Semester 1 and Karin during Semester 2—and we would also be apart for the summers on both ends of that! We knew the upcoming 15 months would be tough—in fact, downright excruciating. But we both felt the relationship was worth it.

Upon arriving at Myrtle Beach, we danced late into the evening at Fat Harold's, a favourite swing dancing establishment. That night, we took a walk next to the ocean. During a break in conversation, Karin turned to me and said, "I don't mind if it happens soon or if we wait until senior year, but at some point I want you to be the first person to kiss me". At that moment I think the waves stopped, the stars held their breath, and the other beachgoers faded into a blur. I took Karin's moonlit face in my hands and softly but firmly pressed my lips to hers. Ecstasy! This was the way it was supposed to be. This was good and true and beautiful.

But we still waited to say, "I love you".

Breaking Up Is Hard to Do

One of the more noticeable aspects of the Jewish Betrothal Story is the role that the couple's parents played. They made the primary decision about whom their son or daughter married and what the conditions of the covenant would be. Thankfully, in the modern West things are different. Karin and I appreciated the freedom to choose each other, but we liked the intentionality and accountability that characterised the process in biblical times.

How could we apply some of that to our relationship? I suggested that we each travel to the other's home that upcoming summer and meet each other's parents.

I had hoped that positive feedback from our folks would confirm our desire to see this relationship through the upcoming year of physical separation. Unfortunately, those visits didn't go as well as we'd hoped. Things were off to a shaky start, and they would only get worse in the months to come.

I spent the fall semester in Colorado Springs, which was spiritually, intellectually and aesthetically stimulating. I met new people and dove into new adventures, like climbing my first "fourteener" (a mountain peak with an elevation of at least 14,000 feet or 4,300 meters). Within a month or two my romantic feelings for Karin began to fade. It took even less time than that for our different communication styles to feed a growing sense of disappointment. I felt emotionally distant from Karin. When we talked by phone we didn't connect very well. This was years before Skype and affordable webcams, so there were no smiles or head tilts to aid our affections.

One day I was sitting inside the radio studio at Focus on the Family. Chuck Colson, the national Christian leader and founder of Prison Fellowship, was the guest. At one point during his interview, Colson challenged any member of the studio audience to answer a very simple, straightforward question: "What is truth?" Gulp. Everyone around me froze. Then the person next to me nudged me toward the microphone. I can't remember my response—only that it referenced C. S. Lewis—but Colson said on air that it was a good answer!

Later that day I got a call from my mom and then a call from my girlfriend ... from high school. They called to congratulate me on the interview that they'd just heard on the radio. But no call came from Karin. I had just survived what I considered an enormous challenge in front of a huge listening audience, interacting with none other than Chuck Colson and James Dobson. Surely that deserved a phone call from Duke! I felt deflated and hurt. My expectations for support and encouragement had veered way off, just as Karin's had a week or two earlier when I failed to respond well to a mixed tape she spent hours making for me. Our love languages weren't gelling.

By Thanksgiving, my frustration had reached a breaking point. I wanted out. I flew to Karin's home in Kansas for the holiday, telling my roommate that by the end of the weekend I'd be single again.

I decided the most opportune time to end the relationship was during a walk around Karin's neighbourhood. We set off, and I remember praying that I would deliver the news firmly but graciously and that Karin would be okay upon receiving it. Thank God for unanswered prayers. I mean that literally—thank the Lord that I never had a chance to follow through on my intentions. Sensing what I was about to do, Karin very bluntly said, "I'm not going to let you break up with me". Things admittedly had been rough between us, but she said our relationship was worth fighting for. We had a lot to work on, and a menacing, even longer-distance relationship loomed before us in the spring. But she asked that we at least hang on until winter break, when we'd be able to see each other again. We could make a final decision at that point. I agreed.

Going the Distance

Karin's early-January visit to my home in New Jersey was the last time we would see each other until late April. She was headed to Vienna, Austria with the university's wind symphony for the entire spring semester. Our time together was sweet, and we rekindled some of what had waned during the previous months apart. But we couldn't ignore what lay just around the corner.

Karin's plane was scheduled to depart from the Baltimore-Washington International Airport. I dreaded the goodbye, but, fortuitously, the flight was delayed for almost two hours. During the wait, we acknowledged that another "change" in our feelings for each other was "likely" (I would have used the words "decrease" and "inevitable", but I didn't want things to get too glum). We found ourselves sharing something in common with Chad and Kayla in the Covenant Love Story: our relationship would need to be based on something deeper than romantic feelings. We couldn't commit to maintain certain emotions; that's not the sort of thing within one's control. We could, however, commit to take certain actions for the duration of our time apart.[35] We could commit to a long-distance relationship until we were back together for our fourth and final year of college, when we could see how things progressed under more normal circumstances. So we found a vacant table, pulled out some paper, and wrote down seven specific acts we would devote ourselves to during our time apart:

1) Praying for each other;

2) Fasting once a week for our relationship;

3) Being honest with each other;

4) Encouraging and helping the other to reach their full potential;

5) Acting in the other's best interest;

6) Honouring the other in their absence as we would in their presence; and

7) Communicating our feelings, thoughts, and experiences regularly through phone calls and letters.

We drafted it in very formal language and even signed and dated both copies. It became known as our Baltimore-Washington Constitution, and I still carry it in my wallet to this day. (See photo, page 70.)

We worked hard that semester on our relationship, and we missed each other terribly. Looking back on it, I think we made great strides in our communication, but I desperately counted down the days for Karin's return.

It was fitting that the semester was capped by another relationship milestone in an airport. On April 20, I arrived early at the terminal and handed out a dozen individual sunflowers to random people waiting at Karin's arrival gate. I also showed them a photo of Karin and asked if they would participate in my celebration of her homecoming. When Karin walked off the jetway and into the terminal, my accomplices handed her the sunflowers, one by one. I took up my post at the end of the receiving line, holding a single rose. We embraced and breathed a sigh of relief. We'd made it!

Finally, "I Love You"

The only thing standing between us and a full senior year together in the same place was the summer. I spent it interning at a think tank in Washington, D.C. while Karin worked for an educational program on Duke's campus. By the end of that summer, I had been pursuing Karin in an exclusive, romantic relationship for about 20 months. There were many moments during that time when we had looked longingly into each other's eyes and said, inaudibly, "I love you". But we hadn't voiced those words aloud. Perhaps this was a side-effect of our "wait until it hurts ... and then some" approach to physical romance. Or perhaps we sensed how much weight these words carry and wanted to safeguard their meaning. For whatever reason, we had saved this powerful phrase for just the right time.

It came during Karin's visit to D.C. on one of my last weekends there. We found ourselves sitting hand-in-hand on a grassy slope in Bethesda, Maryland, moments away from saying "good-bye" for the final time. In a matter of weeks, we'd be back at university, together. The backdrop wasn't the most romantic in the world: the grassy slope overlooked the National Institute of Health. But the timing was right, and so I said aloud what I had wanted to convey to Karin for many months. "I love you."

Again: Ecstasy! This was the way it was supposed to be. This was good and true and beautiful.

Our relationship was prompted by infatuation at first sight, but it had developed into a commitment to love each other through intentional words and deeds. It was a relationship not based on, but assisted by, romantic feelings and physical desires. We had progressed through the first stage of our relationship—desiring intimate, bodily communion—and were ready to commit to serving and giving ourselves to each other for the rest of our lives. We were ready to make the big decision, so we took the natural, sensible next step.

We entered pre-engagement counselling.

4

STAGE 2: STARTING THE PROCESS OF COVENANT MAKING

Engagement

The first stage of the ancient Jewish betrothal process was desiring intimate, bodily communion. This was a hope held not only by the spouses in terms of what their future relationship might become; it was also shared by their parents, who often brought the bride and groom together for that purpose. Once the two families had made clear their desire for marital union, the next stage was entering the process of covenant making, or betrothal (*kiddushin* in Hebrew). Today we call this "getting engaged", but it differs from the ancient meaning of betrothal in significant ways.

Back then, Chad and his father wrote down the terms of the marriage covenant in a document called a *katubah*. (Today some Jewish couples frame their *katubah* and hang it on the wall in their home.) Then, in the presence of several witnesses, Chad and his father discussed these terms with Kayla's father, and she was given an opportunity to accept or reject them as well. This covenantal conversation revealed what both parties understood marriage to be, articulated conditions for its legitimate fulfilment, and outlined the expectations of the spouses. What's important to note is that this detailed discussion took place *before* the two were betrothed.

Signing the *katubah* was a very significant act; beginning at that moment, Chad and Kayla were considered husband and wife. Society would view any infidelity from that point forward as adultery, and it would treat Kayla as a widow if Chad died. Their betrothal was legally binding and could only be broken by a formal divorce.[36]

Although that's not the case today, I liked the fact that this ancient process was taken so seriously in its initial stages. I also appreciated that couples entered into betrothal publically, with family on hand as witnesses. Furthermore, it made a lot of sense that the two parties discussed their understanding of the covenant, along with its terms and expectations, *before* entering it. There was still planning and preparation to attend to after the betrothal, but that had to do with establishing the conditions for the covenant's fulfilment (namely, building a common residence). This sort of planning took place after—and separate from—discussions about the nature of marriage and the spouses' roles within it.

Today the normal route toward marriage follows a different path. After "falling in love", couples typically get engaged in a more private setting, perhaps over a candlelit dinner. (Some pop the question in a very public way, for example, through skywriting or on the jumbotron screen at a sports arena. Yet, even in these cases, their families are not usually present, and the surrounding crowd plays the role of onlooker or well-wisher rather than legal witness to a covenant.) Moreover, if the two do pursue intentional preparation for marriage, it often takes place after the engagement and amidst the rest of the wedding planning. Most importantly, though, today engagement is not typically viewed in terms of entering a covenant. If a couple thinks in terms of covenant at all, they view entering it at their wedding ceremony rather than their engagement.

Preparing Too Late

Influenced by the Jewish betrothal process, Karin and I approached our engagement with great seriousness. In particular, we wanted to recover some of the deliberate accountability and preparation that characterised Chad and Kayla's story. Unfortunately, we knew of no common public rituals or practices to guide modern young couples who are about to "get hitched".

The closest thing we knew of was premarital counselling. I understood this as an opportunity to talk through the meaning and challenges of marriage. Furthermore, it allows a third party to observe the couple's communication styles and relational dynamics. If pastors or priests run the sessions, they are also well-positioned to equip the couple with a theological understanding of family, sex, and marriage. What's more, they can advise couples about whether or not they're ready to take up this high calling.

We knew people in our church who had gone through premarital counselling, but a large percentage of the broader population avoids it. One study found that only 27% of married couples seek premarital counselling.[37] Furthermore, pastors report that the couples who do receive counselling usually allow time for only two or three sessions, each lasting about an hour.[38] If those statistics are true, I find them rather troubling. Think about it: we prepare more for school exams and sports competitions than we do for marriage. Yet marriage is life-long and has the power to make us happier or more miserable than almost anything else in the world.

Another concern is the unwillingness of many couples to submit to pastoral authority in premarital counselling. Rather than seeking out their church's understanding, fiancés often seem to presume that the meaning of marriage is something they get to determine. Our culture encourages couples to believe that *they* should decide what kind of obligations marriage entails and how binding those obligations will be. (This view is sometimes reflected in the desire to write their own wedding vows.) If a couple doesn't want to follow their pastor's counsel, they can simply find another one down the street to perform the ceremony.

In my opinion, though, the biggest problem with premarital counselling today lies in its timing: *premarital* typically translates into *after engagement and right before the wedding*. Thus, at the point that many engaged couples enter such counselling, they've already set the wedding date. They've already booked the ceremony and reception sites. They've already made the news public and likely already sent invitations to every important person in their lives. He's already paid for a ring, and she's already fallen in infatuation with it. And she and her mother have already seen her in *the* dress.

That's a lot of subtle pressure, on the couple and the pastor, to have the sessions turn out a success.

It's terribly disappointing to call off or postpone a wedding; it would be extremely embarrassing if this were due to unforeseen disagreements that arose in counselling. "Surely", the fiancés tell themselves, "once we're married we can work out a budget or come to agreement on whether or not to have kids. After all, we love each other, and that will get us through anything!" The couple, therefore, may likely proceed according to plan, complete their counselling, and set out to live happily ever after. Unfortunately, divorce statistics reveal that such an outcome is more easily hoped for than achieved.

Several years ago, a licensed social worker surveyed nearly 1,000 divorced women about their previous marriages; 30 percent of the respondents admitted to marrying despite serious doubts they had long before the wedding day.[39] That's a lot of pain and heartbreak. One wonders how many of those relationships could have benefited from a more strategic approach to counselling and accountability up front.

Sadly, our culture provides dating couples no process of planning or training prior to popping the question. Even most churches lack deliberate services, liturgies, or catechetical processes for training and evaluating couples moving toward engagement. In the modern West, we view getting engaged as the start—rather than the end result—of a process of intentional, church-guided examination and discernment.

With the Jewish Betrothal Story in mind, Karin and I began to think differently about engagement. We viewed it as a time when the questioning and decision making should have already been completed. Leading up to the wedding, there are too many other pressures in play that can sway the outcome. The logical implication of this view is that intentional discussions about marriage need to occur before getting down on one knee.

We therefore asked our pastor to lead us in pre-engagement counselling.

Pre-Engagement Counselling

He looked at us a bit puzzled and said, "What do you mean by pre-engagement counselling?"

"Just take us through the same process you lead couples through in premarital counselling sessions", we responded. "If you discuss with them sex, money, communication, in-laws, and parenting within marriage, then discuss those things with us."

He asked, "How long do you want it to go?"

"As long as you think it needs to", we answered.

"And then … ?"

"Then tell us whether or not you think we should marry."

I don't think our pastor was used to couples voluntarily submitting to that kind of authority. But he agreed and put us through our paces the rest of our senior year.

God truly blessed us through his guidance; he shared deep biblical wisdom and down-to-earth advice about marriage. His counselling was personal as well as practical. He delivered it with humour and sensitivity but didn't shy away from areas where we needed improvement.

In addition to unpacking the Scriptures with us, our pastor had us create a sample budget for our first year of marriage. He also watched us handle disagreements and counselled us about how we fight with each other. At times, we left his office in tears, which I've come to view as an almost necessary component of good pre-engagement counselling. (Tip to any couple in counselling: keep at it until you have at least one meaningful fight in front of your pastor. It's invaluable to get responsible, third-party feedback from that.)

During this time, a family ministry organisation hosted a marriage renewal weekend nearby. Spouses enrolled to hear presentations on healing and bolstering their relationships. Believing that one cannot prepare too much for something as important as marriage, Karin and I decided to attend the conference. We were the youngest couple there by far. Upon hearing that we weren't yet engaged but wanted to learn how to approach the most typical struggles in marriage, other participants exclaimed, "How we wish we'd learned these lessons before getting married!"

Pre-engagement planning and preparation makes a lot of sense. It can, however, take place too early. If couples haven't yet developed a deep level of intimacy, or if they or their relationship lack the necessary maturity, it can be unhealthy to begin taking serious steps toward marriage. The decision to start intentional preparation for engagement should be made with careful discernment and input from others who know you well—perhaps including your parents, mentors, friends, and pastor or priest.

Karin and I sought the counsel of these voices during the second semester of our senior year. They were unfamiliar with the idea of pre-engagement counselling and asked lots of questions about it. Ultimately, though, they agreed that we were ready to "engage" in it.

A few months later, our pastor called and said he thought the counselling had gone well; he believed we were well prepared for marriage and he'd be willing to perform the wedding when we got to that point.

Needless to say, I knew that the formal proposal wouldn't come as a surprise to Karin. I could still be creative, though, in how I approached it. I wanted it to be memorable and special. Mostly, I wanted it to symbolise the beginning of the commitment we would enter at that moment. I wanted our engagement to participate in the larger story of covenant marriage in the biblical tradition.

But what, exactly, is a covenant?

Covenant Identity

Following the signing of the *katubah* in the Jewish betrothal process, Chad would say to Kayla, "I am your husband, and you are my wife". Often times she responded in kind, "I am your wife, and you are my husband". Although short and simple, these words expressed something very significant about the nature of a covenant that distinguishes it from a mere contract.

Before studying the Jewish Betrothal Story, I presumed that a covenant is simply a glorified promise—a contract on steroids. I had heard Christians say, "marriage is a covenant, not just a contract", but I didn't know what that difference was all about.

As I came to find out, covenants are solemn and binding agreements demanding the commitment of both parties to its established terms.[40] What's especially interesting is that, unlike a typical contract, entering a covenant forms a quasi-familial relationship; it's a way of extending the bond of blood beyond one's kin. Covenants bring about the kind of commitment and responsibility to others that we find in a healthy family.[41]

Furthermore, whereas people entered contracts mainly to exchange goods and services, parties to a covenant exchanged something deeper: *personal identities*. According to one scholar, underlying all covenants is the idea, "I am yours, you are mine".[42] The parties agree to bind themselves to, and be identified with, each other from that point forward.

After Chad and Kayla identified themselves as the other's spouse, it was time to seal the betrothal. To accomplish this, Chad poured a cup of wine and offered it to Kayla, saying, "This cup represents a covenant in blood". As a sign of accepting the offer to enter this covenant, she sipped from the cup.

The wine represented the blood of an animal, which was often sprinkled at covenant-making or covenant-"cutting" ceremonies. (*Berith*, the Hebrew word for covenant, stems from a word meaning "to cut".) By shedding an animal's blood and separating the carcass in two, the parties essentially said to each other, in the presence of God, "May the same be done to me if I fail to keep this covenant". This was serious business! In short, sipping from the cup of wine was a way of enacting a solemn oath. In Scripture, covenants were made with the swearing of oaths that include certain blessings and curses for fidelity and infidelity.

"So Help Me God"

When forming a biblical covenant, the importance of swearing an oath cannot be overstated. The oath gives the covenant's commitments and responsibilities their binding validity, for if they are broken, a divine curse will result. This further separates covenants from mere contracts—the former invoke God's punishment on the unfaithful party.

In our society people still swear allegiance under divine authority when taking up certain public responsibilities. This is true, for example, in the military. Mounted on the wall inside Bancroft Hall at the United States Naval Academy is a plaque displaying the words of the seaman's (called "midshipman") oath of office. Every midshipman must swear this oath to be commissioned in the Navy. The oath's final words appear in enlarged lettering: "SO HELP ME GOD".

Invoking God's help also anchors the oaths taken by policemen, doctors, government authorities, and judges. These figures all bear great authority and responsibility, serve the common good in a crucial way, and deal with situations where life and death are on the line.

The same is true of husbands and wives.

Marriage is meant to be a life-long relationship that carries great authority and responsibility, advances the common good of society, and has the power to bring about and sustain new life. Therefore, it is appropriate that spouses also publicly swear an oath upon entering their covenant. In biblical times this entailed sipping from a cup of wine; today you will hear some wedding vows end with "so help me God".[43]

In the typical Jewish betrothal process, Chad also presented Kayla with a betrothal gift (*terhatum*), either in the form of money or a ring made of precious metal. Finally, the ceremony may have concluded with the families celebrating a betrothal meal together. This was a fitting custom, for sharing food has the power to symbolise and foster relational bonds among those gathered together.[44]

Her Father's Blessing

With this tradition in mind, I started to set engagement plans in motion in late March of Karin's and my senior year. First, I selected a ring; but I wanted to get a female opinion before making the final purchase. While in town for a track and field competition, my sister Natalie accompanied me to the local jewellery store to check out the diamond. I couldn't afford a big one, but Natalie approved of my selection.

Several weeks later, I chose the proposal date and location: the night of April 27 on the top of the Duke Chapel tower. In each of the four semesters I had taught the *Narnia* class, I'd taken students there to discuss *Prince Caspian*. I think the lady in charge of the tower elevator thought I'd be doing the same this time. When she saw me coming on the 26th, she just handed me the key, no questions asked. I said nothing but, "thank you".

When the 27th arrived, things didn't start out so smoothly. I'd made several attempts to talk to Karin's dad about the proposal, but because he was travelling earlier that week, I hadn't been able to reach him. I tried calling again that morning, but, again, no luck. To make matters worse, rain poured down all day and the forecast predicted it would continue all night. I had to return the elevator key the next morning, so there was no turning back. I decided that, when I ascended the tower, I would take a big blue tarp and construct a temporary canopy at its top. (See photo, page 71.) I wasn't happy about it, but it would have to do.

The situation got a little brighter at that afternoon's *Narnia* session. Karin came to the class sporting a style I refer to as *debonair*. (In high school I started "Debonair Day"; on the first Tuesday of the month guys wore jeans, dress shirts and ties and girls wore jeans and blazers.) Karin knew I liked that look and for some reason decided to wear jeans and a blazer that day.

She also mentioned in passing that she had talked to her parents on the phone before class. They were home—my window of opportunity! I said goodbye to Karin and raced back to my dorm to make the call. Karin's mom answered and informed me that Karin's dad was out back on the tractor. I insisted on speaking to him ASAP. She knew what was coming; I could hear it in her voice as she called him to the phone. After I disclosed my desires for that evening, her dad said something like, "make sure you don't get nervous and forget your lines". That was the green light I'd been seeking. I quickly changed into my dress shirt, tie, and best blue jeans and headed for the chapel.

Our Engagement

My roommate, Will, came with me. He was a necessary part of the plan and played his role to perfection. He accompanied me in the chapel tower elevator to the top, dropped me off and then proceeded back down with the elevator key. (The key activated the power switch, so the person riding the elevator had to have the key present.) I needed a way to get the key to Karin and then to get her to the top of the tower by herself. The plan was to convince her that I had created a scavenger hunt, sort of like the show *Amazing Race*, with the first destination being the chapel tower. Upon delivering

Karin the clue and the elevator key, Will would take off so that she'd have to proceed to the top on her own.

I prayed the plan would work. If it didn't, I'd have no way to get back down! Harkening back to Karin's airport homecoming one year earlier, I placed a row of sunflowers leading from the door of the elevator, across the walkway overlooking the carillon of massive church bells, up a small flight of stairs, and out onto the platform. There I built the canopy and under it placed a chair, surrounded by candle luminaries. Nearby I placed a chalice, a bottle of wine, and a glass bowl and towel. Finally, as the rain continued, I held my breath and plugged in a portable stereo, hoping I wouldn't get electrocuted in the process. Then, all I could do was wait and wonder.

Would Karin understand the scavenger hunt clue? Would she know how to operate the rickety, old-fashioned elevator? At the top, would she remember to take the key out of the switch before closing the door and automatically locking us out of our only way back to the ground?

After what seemed like hours, I detected the mechanical growl of the rusty elevator. It was music to my ears. The plan was working! Karin made it to the top and a minute later was standing at the door to the platform holding the key and the sunflowers. I was waiting with a single rose.

I brought her by the hand to the chair and invited her to take her place on the throne. I then knelt on bended knee and explained how much she meant to me and how I wanted to spend the rest of my life loving her. I declared that I wanted to be her husband; I asked if she would be my wife.

She smiled and said, "Yes!"

Borrowing from the ancient Jewish custom, I then poured wine into a crystal chalice and said, "This cup represents a covenant in blood". I offered it to her, and she gladly took a sip. Next, after slipping the ring onto her finger, I wanted to demonstrate the kind of active, servant love to which we had just committed. I took the glass bowl and towel and washed her feet. This is how Christ loved his disciples during the Last Supper the night he established his new covenant with them.[45]

Finally, I led Karin out to an elevated part of the platform. On the highest spot of the tower on which to stand, I played a number of songs that were special in our relationship. We held each other close and danced in the rain. The huge spotlights that illumine the chapel each night shone up at us, and they cast our silhouettes against the low-hanging clouds. It was a truly magical and profound moment.

As we swayed to the music, I sensed that we were taking our place in a larger dance—we were tapping into something ancient and solemn and right. This was the goal romantic impulses were designed to serve. This was good and true and beautiful.

We held hands, kissed and exclaimed, "I love you". With the cup with which we had sealed engagement, we toasted the Author of our love story.

Our Relationship Constitution

I, Karin K Stoskopf, in recognition of my exclusive relationship with Ryan Messmore, in order to foster our growth together, do hereby on this third day of January in the year of our Lord 1996 solemnly commit to the following:

To lift Ryan up before the Lord regularly in prayer,

To fast once a week, remembering our relationship,

To be honest with Ryan at all times,

To encourage Ryan, enabling him to reach his full potential,

To do my best to always act in Ryan's best interests,

To honor Ryan in his absence as I would in his presence,

To communicate my feelings, thoughts, and experiences with Ryan faithfully, including some of my prayers.

MAY OUR RELATIONSHIP ALWAYS GLORIFY HIM.

Karin K Stoskopf   Ryan S. Messmore

Karin K Stoskopf 5/14/96   Ryan S. Messmore 5/14/96

On January 3rd, 1996, while waiting at the airport for Karin's flight to Vienna, Austria, we created our Baltimore-Washington Constitution. We wrote two versions—one from her and one from me—and then we signed both copies. Upon Karin's return later that year, we renewed our commitment by signing them again. I still carry it in my wallet.

Our Engagement

On April 27th, 1997, I proposed to Karin on top of the Duke Chapel. Because it was raining, I used a large tarp to build a tent-like structure for Karin to sit under. She took the elevator up to the bell carillon level, then followed a path of sunflowers that led her outside to the top of the tower. I placed candle luminaries around her chair and offered her a cup of wine to seal the engagement. I then washed Karin's feet and we danced in the rain on the elevated platform (top right of the photo).

15 years later, in 2012, Karin and I took our three kids (Joshua, Christopher, and Katie) back to Duke's campus to share with them a bit of our story.

5

STAGE 3: ESTABLISHING CONDITIONS FOR FULFILMENT
Preparing for Marriage

After entering and sealing their betrothal, a typical couple in the ancient Jewish tradition began establishing the necessary conditions for fulfilling their marriage covenant. What sort of conditions must be in place to help realise the goals and goods of marriage?

The answer has to do with the intended degree of self-giving between spouses: marriage is meant to be the *full* sharing of *entire* lives. The giving is comprehensive—it takes place across all aspects of a relationship. Husbands and wives are called to freely unite in not only their minds and wills but also their bodies, and to commit to share their residence, resources, finances, and future destinies. This is not only because all-inclusive sharing is the natural implication of full self-giving love, but also because of the benefits this sort of commitment provides children.[46] Therefore, fulfilling the marriage covenant requires making sure conditions are in place that foster the full sharing of persons and lives.

In ancient Israel, establishing the conditions for married life primarily had to do with planning for the wedding celebration and preparing a house. Both took place at the homestead of the groom's father. Upon sealing the betrothal, Chad returned there to begin building the bridal chamber (*chuppah*). Custom dictated that its design resemble the Tabernacle of Moses. Scripture scholar Brant Pitre notes that, "according to one rabbi, the measurements of a bridechamber were supposed to match those of the holy of holies", and its decorations were similar to those of the Tabernacle.[47] Given the seriousness surrounding this room's construction, Chad's father had to approve when it was finished and when the wedding would take place. If someone asked Chad about the timing of his wedding, he would customarily reply, "Only my father knows".

Preparing Our Home

Upon beginning the process of entering our covenant (i.e., getting engaged), Karin and I began to establish the conditions for its fulfilment. Preparing for the wedding involved the normal activities: finding the perfect dress for Karin, sending out invitations, placing newspaper announcements, enlisting bridesmaids, groomsmen, and a ring-bearer, registering for gifts, and making endless choices about flowers, decorations, table arrangements, and so forth. At first I attempted to involve myself in these sorts of decisions. It didn't take long, though, to realise that I'd have more success focusing on other things ... like finding furniture for our apartment.

Graduation followed closely on the heels of our April engagement. Karin and I would both be attending graduate school at Duke in the fall, so we decided to spend the summer in Durham. I moved into the cheapest one-bedroom apartment within walking distance of campus. Karin stayed in a friend's place until our December wedding.

Our first apartment was one we'll never forget, full of interesting neighbours, cockroaches, and crime. During my first night there, I slept in a sleeping bag laid on top of a thin mat. With my face so close to the floor, I could smell marijuana and hear passionate, sexual moaning coming from the apartment one floor below. "Good grief", I thought, "this is like living in a TV show!" Things weren't as humorous some months later when the police advised residents of a shooting in the apartment complex's laundry facility.

Was I doing the right thing in bringing Karin into this place? Was I providing a safe, secure home during our first years of marriage? I wasn't so sure, but it was all I could afford. Maybe ancient Jewish families were on to something—building a room onto the family's house didn't seem like such a bad idea after all. But without a car, I needed to be able to walk to class, and this sketchy neighbourhood was much closer to campus than my home in New Jersey.

The task of furnishing the apartment proved relatively simple, and it was much shorter than the year-long process of building a *chuppa*. One nice thing about staying in Durham after graduation was that I inherited the furniture of classmates who were leaving town. Within a week or two, I had accumulated a used couch, recliner, desk, bookshelf, TV stand, kitchen table and four chairs. I even rescued a mattress that someone had ditched in the dumpster. I managed for about seven months using old towels in the bathroom and plastic plates and utensils in the kitchen. Things started looking up when the wedding registry gifts began to arrive: nice plates, plush linens, fine china, and picture frames and candlesticks galore! Karin's dad bought a TV to go on the TV stand, and with that, the apartment was complete. The main conditions for fulfilling our covenant had been met.

Well, almost.

There were at least four other preparations that required attention before the wedding.

Common Cents

The first had to do with money. We had heard that financial decisions are the most common source of tension within marriage. Therefore, during our pre-engagement counselling, Karin and I formulated a hypothetical budget in great detail. But planning a budget and actually sticking to it are two very different things. We felt we needed practice.

More importantly, we knew that wealth has the uncanny ability to reflect and even to shape a couple's relationship. Money represents what we value and prioritise; "where your treasure is, there your heart will be also" (Matthew 6:21). How we spend our resources reflects something about our individual character. Karin and I suspected that our willingness to share money with each other would also reflect something about the character of our marriage.

During this season of preparation, I came across a quote by Stanley Hauerwas, my Christian ethics professor in divinity school. In commenting on sexual ethics and marriage, he writes:

> [W]e should not trust our declaration of love unless we are willing to commit ourselves publicly. For there is surely no area where we are more liable to self-deception than in those contexts where love is mixed with sexual desire. ... The problem with the suggestion that sexual expression should be relative to the level of loving commitment is that it is simply too hard to test the latter. I would suggest instead that the form and extent of our sexual expression is best correlated to the extent we are willing to intermix our finances. It may sound terribly unromantic, but I am convinced that one of the best tests of "love" is the extent a couple are willing to share a common economic destiny.[48]

Pretty unromantic, indeed; but Karin and I agreed with his point. We decided not to keep separate accounts upon getting married. To prepare for that, we decided to open a joint bank account when we got engaged. We both still had separate accounts during that time, but we used the common account for shared expenses—things like eating out together, going to movies together, travelling home for the holidays together, and buying small items for the apartment.

Parenting 101

In addition to housing and financial arrangements, preparing for marriage also entails preparing for parenthood. This sort of claim would likely strike Mike as confusing. After all, within modern culture's EPIC Story, having children is an option that people can either pursue or avoid at their own whim. From this perspective, there is no intrinsic connection between marriage and procreation. As a representative of today's dominant narrative, Mike would view marriage as a relationship oriented first and foremost toward his own desires and needs, not those of children. In fact, he may conclude that having kids would cramp his style and hinder his upward mobility. A *Time* magazine cover story captured this attitude with the headline: "The Childfree Life: When having it all means not having children".[49]

But if love is considered the act of giving oneself to another, do things not appear somewhat differently? As an outward-focused gift, it's the nature of love to be given away to another. We see this in the creation of the universe by the God whose very nature is love. As the divine Father and Son eternally give themselves to each other in the power of the Holy Spirit, their unity creates more to love—i.e. creation. Divine love is fruitful and outward focused. Likewise, when a husband and wife love each other in the fullest way possible, they engage in the kind of act that creates more to love— i.e. children. Their love is typically fruitful. It doesn't turn inward upon itself, but moves outward in a family-expanding direction.

Also, remember that covenants are made by the swearing of oaths that include blessings and curses for fidelity and infidelity. We can view children as one of the covenant blessings intended to flow from marital love. Offspring are to be received as gifts, the fruit of faithful self-giving.[50]

Thus, a commitment to marriage is a commitment to *the kind of family life* that concretely embodies self-giving love. There is an intrinsic link between marriage and openness to children.[51] Rather than merely a choice, there's a deep inner logic connecting the marital promise and procreation.

This connection to children is the primary reason why governments have traditionally regulated marriages but not other kinds of intimate relationships, such as friendships. Have you ever wondered why the state got involved in romantic relationships in the first place, or why sexual partners would ever allow—let alone call for—it to do so?[52] According to Bertrand Russell, the British Nobel laureate and self-ascribed agnostic, "it is through children alone that sexual relations become of importance to society, and worthy to be taken cognizance of by a legal institution".[53] Likewise, others have argued that governments would not have institutionalised marriage if humans reproduced asexually and were self-sufficient at birth.[54] The reason governments have traditionally done so is because marriage is the kind of relational structure that generates future citizens and commits their moms and dads to their upbringing.

Karin and I figured that, like marriage itself, one cannot prepare too much for the task of raising baby humans. So, while engaged, we enrolled in a parenting class offered by our church. As was the case at the marriage conference we had attended before getting engaged, we were the youngest couple by far in this group of parents. In fact, on the first day of the class we received many glances that communicated, "Do you have any news we should know about?" But we simply wanted to learn from those with experience how best to succeed in—or, better, survive—the wonderful adventure called parenthood. Whether it was in discussing discipline or tips for getting babies to sleep through the night, I think the biggest overall lesson we learned was that parenting requires the dedication and cooperation of entire lives!

A Community of Support (Even Concerning Sex)

Chad and Kayla lived in a society in which cooperation and help with parenting was readily available. Rather than moving off by themselves to tackle life on their own, their marriage was likely embedded in a family and a family's home. Chad and Kayla could look to their own parents and extended family members for guidance, tips, and practical assistance in cooking, shopping, and watching their kids after nights with little sleep.

Even if a couple cannot have children, marriage isn't the sort of life-long commitment that's easily undertaken as a "lone ranger" couple. We will all struggle to successfully give ourselves to another—continuously sharing our finances, residence, forgiveness, and so forth—if we rely solely on our own will power. We need people to encourage us and help keep us accountable in our marriage when the going gets tough.

In Leo Tolstoy's classic novel *Anna Karenina*, a priest prays during Levin and Kitty's wedding ceremony that the Lord might "grant them perfect love, peace, and help". Levin thinks to himself:

> "How did they guess that it's help, precisely help, that one needs? ... What do I know? What can I achieve in this fearful business," he thought, "without help? Yes, it is precisely help that I need now." ... Levin was increasingly feeling that all his ideas about marriage, his dreams about how he would organize his life—that

all this had been childish and that it was something he had not yet understood and now understood even less, even though it was happening to him; there were shudders rising higher and higher in his chest, and unruly tears springing into his eyes.[55]

This "fearful business" of marriage that requires help extends even to a couple's sex life. Sex bonds marriages together, and marriages are the foundations of communities. Therefore, as Wendell Berry has argued, sex is not merely private but has significance for the health of a larger society. "For sex is not and cannot be any individual's 'own business' ... Sex, like any other necessary, precious, and volatile power that is commonly held, is everybody's business."[56]

What are the practical implications of claiming that sex and marriage are linked to neighbourhood and community accountability? Among other things, it means we shouldn't separate our sexual lives from the support that a larger community—especially one that lives by the Christian story—can offer. As *Real Sex* author, Lauren Winner, suggests, it means cultivating the kinds of relationships with friends in which we can open up our day-to-day lives to them. To grant permission to others within a Christian community to ask us about our sexual relationships is "not to imagine a world where Mr. Married offers a Christianized version of locker-room chat with his buddies in the pews. It is not to imply that my married friends need to regale me with the details every time they make love". It is, rather, to recognise that members of the Christian community have an obligation to help each other with sexual sin as well as "the complicated emotional and physical thickets one can find oneself in when one is having sex. It is to urge Christians to speak frankly to one another about the realities of chastity, about the thrills and tediums of married sex, about the rich meanings inherent in being sexual persons who live in bodies".[57]

In light of this, another important way to prepare for marriage is to gather friends and community members around you who can assist with the burdens of married and family life. This includes not only emotional support but physical and financial support as well. A couple considering marriage would do well to find a supportive community, like a small group or a mentoring couple at a local church, who can commit with them to work toward a healthy union.

An Unanticipated Issue

For Karin and me, there was a fifth area requiring preparation before the wedding, and it was a big one. It had to do with the question of natural family planning (NFP)—i.e., abstaining from having sex during times when pregnancy is most likely.

This topic first came up during our second year in college (after our first dinner but before holding hands). Karin and I found a book of questions intended to foster conversation between couples.[58] Often we would open the book, read aloud a single question, and then spend the next two hours sharing ideas and learning more about each other. Somewhere between our political views, attitudes about cleanliness, and preferred vacation destinations, we happened upon several questions about starting a family and the desired number of children.

That brought up a conversation regarding artificial contraception.

I voiced the first three thoughts that came to my head: 1) opposition to contraception is just a Catholic concern, and we weren't Catholic; 2) there's no moral difference between NFP (which the Catholic Church approves) and artificial contraception (which the Catholic Church disapproves), for both are means of avoiding pregnancy; and 3) if artificial interference with the body is wrong, then so is taking headache medicine, which is ridiculous. Karin agreed. It took us about 90 seconds to dismiss the issue and move to the next question.

The issue didn't surface again until the following year (the final summer of our long-distance relationship). I interned in the social policy department at a Washington, D.C. think tank, and my primary assignment involved researching the effects of no-fault divorce on women and children. During a discussion about marriage, my supervisor mentioned contraception. It took about 90 seconds for him to undercut the three initial objections that Karin and I had mentioned to each other.

First, as a matter of history, contraception has not been merely a Catholic concern. In fact, no Protestant denomination supported artificial contraception until 1930.[59] I was amazed to learn that Martin Luther, John Calvin, John Wesley, and many other Protestant heroes had roundly condemned artificial contraception before that.[60] How could I so easily dismiss this as a "Catholic issue" when fewer than 70 years earlier my church *along with every other Christian denomination* had declared it immoral?[61] I also learned that the Catholic Church doesn't oppose contraception because she's against all means of avoiding pregnancy[62] and all things artificial. The deepest question isn't whether a product is natural or man-made, but what purposes it serves or severs. In other words, the concern is that contraception *intentionally*, rather than merely *artificially*, severs a significant purpose of sex (i.e. procreation), while NFP doesn't.[63]

I was intrigued and a bit surprised at my lack of understanding. I had to be honest and admit that I'd never really thought about artificial contraception as a moral issue to which I should pay much attention. I grew up simply assuming that artificial contraception was morally appropriate and that my future wife and I would most likely practice it.

With my roadblocks out of the way, I was willing to consider a substantial argument. My supervisor gave me an article having to do with the effects of intentionally separating the pleasure of sex from the purpose of procreation and blocking the latter, which began to change my mind. (I refer to it as "that darn article", and I outline how it shaped my thinking in the Appendix.) I reread it several times, sensing that I had encountered a coherent case that I couldn't easily dismiss. It seemed reasonable, but its implications were huge. I call it "that darn article" because accepting its viewpoint would mean that I'd have to alter the way I respond to perhaps the strongest and most pleasurable physical drive known to humans. But I couldn't deny the logic.[64]

I left Washington, D.C. in 1996 with a much different moral and sexual framework than I encountered during my time there with Mike as a high school student. As a thank-you gift at the end of my internship, I gave my supervisor a small compass. I told him that he had pointed my thinking—and life—in a new direction.

So I set off back to Durham to tell Karin ... and almost ran our entire relationship off the tracks!

The Talk

What we refer to now as "the talk" took place on a sunny afternoon outside the music building on campus. We had made it through a 15-month long-distance relationship, and we were about to enter pre-engagement counselling. Everything was moving in the right direction when, without warning, I naively turned to Karin and declared, "Artificial contraception is wrong and all the objections we had to it don't hold water".

She was caught off guard and remained silent as I proceeded to bombard her with philosophical distinctions and technical terminology. All Karin could think at that moment was how she wanted to slap me and run away as fast as she could.

This was a big issue for a couple moving closer and closer to marriage. Karin heard the words "we should practice natural family planning" as "you should give up any hope of having a career so you can raise at least 12 kids". It was a potential deal-breaker, and I had handled it with the delicacy and sensitivity of a pregnant rhinoceros.

I apologised and suggested that we take a step back from discussing the issue. In fact, I proposed that we not talk about it again until she was ready to do so. Whether that was in five days or five months, I wanted her to take as much time as she needed to think and pray about it. (This is another reason why it's good to discuss such issues before getting engaged, and especially before the wedding date is set in stone.) I didn't wish to impose my arguments upon Karin. I wanted her to feel free to do her own research, find her own articles, and talk to her own friends and mentors. In the meantime, I would take a fresh look at the issue as well, trying to view it less as a philosophical question and more as a decision that could have huge implications for a family.

A few weeks later, Karin told me her decision that ... she didn't want to use artificial contraception. She also wanted to learn more about NFP. I felt a deep sense of joy, but not because she had come to agree with a certain viewpoint. Instead, I realised that I was in a serious relationship with someone I admired and respected more each day, who was willing to think deeply about important issues and make sacrifices for her understanding of the truth. I had found a beautiful young woman who didn't run away when the going got tough. An issue that had the potential to bring the whole house of cards crashing down ended up clarifying why I wanted to enter a covenant with this particular partner.

Learning the Signs

Thus, as we prepared the conditions to fulfil our covenant, we looked for information about practicing NFP.

We knew of its less-than-stellar reputation. We had heard all the typical jokes, such as, "What do you call a couple practicing NFP? Parents". If we were going to take this approach, we wanted to find out as much about it as possible. We also wanted to give Karin a lot of practice tracking her fertility before we got married and started having sex. Unfortunately, we couldn't find anybody in town offering NFP classes. So, we made an hour-long drive to participate in a series of classes run by the Catholic Diocese in a neighbouring city. We weren't Catholic at that point, but the teacher allowed us to sit in along with several other young couples.

The method of choice is often called the "ovulation method" and involves monitoring a woman's ovulatory signs throughout the course of her monthly cycle.[65] Karin learned how to do this (which takes about five seconds several times each day) and how to chart the results on a calendar. My role was to remind Karin to check her signs each day.

Fortunately, we had about seven months for Karin to get comfortable with this method. Tracking all this greatly eased our minds once we got married.

Thankfully, NFP has worked perfectly for us all nineteen years of our marriage.[66] I can also attest that it was after we started practicing it that we came to realise one of the surprising reasons for doing so: great anticipation for sex![67]

Premarital Sex

The eight months from our engagement to our wedding were a very busy time. Karin and I not only studied in graduate school but also established the conditions for fulfilling our covenant, including furnishing an apartment, joining finances, learning parenting skills and monitoring NFP.

We found this season of preparation to be both more fun and more challenging than anticipated. We had already wrestled with most of the big issues before engagement, so we were very confident about our relationship. This provided a certain peace of mind and allowed us to enjoy being engaged.

On one occasion, Karin and her friends dined at the restaurant in which I worked over the summer. We decided to play a joke on my fellow wait staff. They knew I was engaged, but, having never met Karin, they didn't know what she looked like. When she walked in, they thought she was a random customer. Back in the kitchen, I told the other staff how hot I thought the blonde at table 12 was, and that I sensed she was flirting with me. Then I asked a fellow waitress to slip that blonde my number. The waitress looked at me in disbelief, but she did it anyway. Karin played along as the flirtatious new customer until, upon getting ready to leave, we came clean about her true identity. It probably wasn't the best witness we could have provided, but it was the most entertaining thing that happened during my job all summer.

What was challenging about engagement was avoiding premarital sex. A typical Friday night found us watching a movie together alone in my apartment. The desire to sleep with each other was fierce; we experienced the urge to "Netflix and chill" before it was a thing. The fact that we were already engaged made it especially tempting.[68] We were committed to each other in pretty much every possible way. We even shared a bank account. Why not express our level of intimacy and commitment through sex?

I was aware of the Christian belief that sex before marriage is wrong, but the only justification I'd heard for this is that, "the Bible says so". But if you ask, "Why does the Bible say so?" you don't often get a very thoughtful response. I wanted a good answer. Why did God establish this particular moral norm against premarital sex, which the Bible conveys?

During the first semester of graduate school, my class with Hauerwas helped. His approach to ethics differs from the one promoted by the authors of the article I had read the previous summer. Whereas those authors took a natural law approach, focusing primarily on the intrinsic goods and natural meaning of certain acts, Hauerwas mainly focused on the way certain acts shape a community. For example, in his book *A Community of Character*, he writes, "prior to the issue of whether premarital or extramarital sexual intercourse is wrong is the question of character: What kind of people do you want to encourage? Hidden in the question of 'What ought we to do?' is always the prior question 'What ought we to be?'"[69]

That got me asking some additional questions. How would certain approaches to sex form me as a person? Would having premarital sex help or hinder me in developing the virtues (like patience and faithfulness) of a good husband? (Such questions also apply to contraception. For example, even if I were to doubt that procreation is intrinsic to the nature of a particular sexual act, how would using contraception shape my thinking about—and my disposition toward—comprehensive, self-giving love?[70])

I had heard a lot from other Christians about how our thoughts and beliefs shape our actions, but Hauerwas' class convinced me that the influence runs the other way as well. That is, our practices can influence our attitudes, desires, and expectations. I wanted to make sure that the actions that Karin and I took during our engagement would shape a healthy understanding of and desire for married love.

A Footnote on Fooling Around

In *Mere Christianity*, C. S. Lewis claims that the problem with sexual intercourse outside marriage is that:

> those who indulge in it are trying to isolate one kind of union (the sexual) from all the other kinds of union which were intended to go along with it and make up the total union. The Christian attitude does not mean that there is anything wrong about sexual pleasure, any more than about the pleasure of eating. It means that you must not isolate that pleasure and try to get it by itself, any more than you ought to try to get the pleasure of taste without swallowing and digesting, by chewing things and spitting them out again.[71]

The idea that certain kinds of union and pleasure are "intended to go along with" other kinds of union greatly influenced my thinking. In a footnote to *A Community of Character*, I came across another quote that echoed this claim and unpacked it even further. It was by Mennonite theologian John Howard Yoder, who suggests that the ethical question concerning fooling around before marriage is:

> whether true love can be honest ... [and] true ... if it dodges the honest *outward expressions which are its normal social form*. ... Therefore what is questionable about 'premarital sex' is ... that the maintenance of secrecy, the avoidance of legality, the postponement of common residence and finances, the withholding of public pledge, constitute both a handicap for the marriage's success and *prima facie* evidence that the love is not true. ... It is not that the hasty youngsters sin against backward cultural mores ... it is that they sin against themselves, their lives and their marriage, by depriving their love of the social consummative, the orderly cohabitative, the

fresh air, without which it is stunted or amputated.[72]

I thought long and hard about the claim that true sexual love has a *normal social form*. That form is a comprehensive, multi-faceted union that calls for complete devotion as well as the sharing of time and space and projects and commitments.[73] This is also the form of union that is suited for raising children—the natural fruit of sex. God created sexual love to thrive within this sort of context, a context in which couples pursue legal recognition, common residence, shared finances, public pledge, and (I would add) the joint adventure of raising kids. Outside of that form, says Yoder, sexual love is stunted and amputated. That's why the Bible presents marriage as the proper boundaries for sex—not because God is a prude, but because He wants love to thrive.

There are reasons why our churches and many societies throughout human history have held to this moral conviction against pre-marital sex. It's not just one of those "backward cultural mores"; there's a substantial ethical difference between the state of being married and the state of about-to-be married. Even on the day before marriage, and even if the couple is already living together, their relationship lacks the public pledge and the church's official witness that are meant to occur at the wedding—and meant for the couple's own benefit.

We wanted our love, our moral character, and our sex life to flourish. So, while we were engaged, I drove Karin home each Friday night after our movie ended. We were convinced that sex would be most fulfilling when placed within a larger context of publicly sanctioned commitment.

The Jewish Betrothal Story provides another insight on pursuing sexual intimacy before marriage, which has to do with the relationship between sex and covenant.

6

STAGE 4: CONSUMMATING THE MARRIAGE

Sex

In the Jewish Betrothal Story, after agreeing on the terms of the covenant, sealing it with a cup of wine, and establishing the conditions for its fulfilment, the couple moved to the crucial stage of consummating it sexually.

At a time approved by his father, Chad, along with his family and friends, would make his way to Kayla's home to claim her as his bride. Kayla would have been alerted as to the day of the wedding so she could prepare properly. On that day, her friends and mother helped her with a ritual bath (called a *mikveh*) that symbolised spiritual cleansing. Then they anointed her with perfumed oils and assisted her into her wedding garments, which included a veil worn over her face.[74] After that, because they didn't know the precise hour of Chad's arrival, they kept watch.[75]

According to Jewish custom, Chad dressed like a priest on this special day, wearing a seamless tunic.[76] His garment was scented with frankincense and myrrh, and, if he could afford it, he wore a gold crown.[77] As the groom's party approached, the groomsman, known as the "friend of the groom", ran ahead and announced Chad's arrival by blowing a ram's horn (*shofar*).

Both parties then made their way back to Chad's father's house in a very noteworthy procession.[78] Kayla, who wore a crown on her head as well,[79] was transported in a carriage lifted up on poles (*aperion*).[80] By custom, the two were referred to as "king" and "queen" for a day, tying them to the first husband and wife (Adam and Eve), who reigned over the animals (Genesis 1:28). This procession was held in very high regard and took precedence over all other traffic they encountered along the way.[81] Invited guests were allowed to join the procession along the dark streets and then enter the groom's father's house, but only if they had with them a torch or lamp[82] and the appropriate wedding clothes.[83]

Upon arriving at Chad's father's house, the couple stood under a canopy or tent and received a blessing. The wedding ceremony (*nisu'in*) also included several familiar components. The couple again heard the covenant document read aloud, again spoke the covenant formula ("Today I have become your husband, and you have become my wife"), and again sipped wine from the same cup with which they sealed their betrothal. Chad and Kayla then went into the private bridechamber (*chuppah*) to consummate the marriage sexually.[84] This was the time of the *apokalypsis*, a word which literally means "lifting of the veil".[85] Chad's friend guarded the room and, upon hearing through the door from the groom that the act was complete, happily announced to all present: "It is consummated!"

It was very important to be able to prove not only that the marriage had been consummated but also that the bride was a virgin. This condition was often written into the terms of the covenant document itself. For this reason, elderly women in the bride's family would recover from the bridechamber the couple's bed sheets, which, if she was a virgin, would likely be stained with blood. If the groom turned around and falsely accused the bride in public of not being a virgin, she could present the blood-stained sheets in her defence.[86]

The newlyweds spent seven continuous days inside the bridechamber. The families celebrated together during this time, and when Kayla and Chad emerged from the bridechamber, a final wedding supper was held on the seventh day.[87]

The Role of Sex in the Story

This elaborate story is a world away from the script directing today's wedding culture. If a tornado could somehow transport Kayla to the present, she'd feel very out of sorts. She'd likely sense the sort of disconnect that moved Dorothy to exclaim, "We're not in Kansas anymore!" Although Karin and I would get married in Kansas, we were intrigued enough to want to incorporate some of Kayla's ancient traditions into our wedding. (See below.)

I was most intrigued with the different role that the couple's sexual union plays in the Covenant Love Story. It's part of the wedding process itself, not just something the couple does back in their hotel after the wedding. In fact, sex seems to be necessary for the whole thing. It plays a significant purpose; it accomplishes something with legal implications.

What is the role of sex in this story? What exactly does it accomplish?

For many, procreation might come to mind. By the time Karin and I got engaged, we believed not only that sex was naturally oriented to having children but also that God created women to be infertile for a majority of days each month. That suggested to us that God must have intended sex to accomplish something in addition to procreation. But what? Others might answer, "uniting the couple in intimacy". Sex certainly has this unitive power and purpose as well, which is a wonderful thing. But most people who have had sex, especially if they have kids and a busy schedule, know that it isn't an emotionally deep experience every time. (In a vintage remark, Hauerwas notes that, "More mundane behavior ... can often be more intimate and significant as an expression of love" than "making the clumsy gestures" involved in sex. And, "We quite properly would sometimes prefer to read a book"![88]) Moreover, in the Jewish Betrothal Story, there's a chance that the couple may not have been physically or emotionally attracted to each other. In that case, their sexual experiences may not have been the most intimate of occasions.

So what, then, did God create sex to do each time?

The answer provided in the ancient Jewish Betrothal Story is to *consummate and renew a marriage covenant.* Sex is intended as covenant ratification and renewal, even if it results neither in conception nor in intimate feelings each and every time.

A Consummate Performance

Growing up, I had heard of the word "consummate", but I really didn't have a good grasp of its meaning. The dictionary definition has to do with *fulfilling, finishing or summing up*, or *making complete or perfect*. To consummate a covenant is to bring its establishment to completion or to enact it to the full. The *intention* to unite two persons in marriage is ratified and sealed at betrothal, which even forms a binding legal relationship. There's a level of union, though, that's not enacted or completed in betrothal; at that stage the process of uniting the couple has not yet reached its full end or *telos*. In its most concrete form, uniting takes place through consummation.

I came to understand this better through learning about a

special kind of sentence called a *performative*. In school we learn that sentences can function either as questions, statements, commands, or exclamations. ("Whose sword is this?" is a question; "The sword belongs to Sir Lancelot" is a statement; "Hand that sword to me quickly" is a command; and "Ouch!" is an exclamation.) We're often less familiar with the kind of utterances called *performatives*. A performative is a statement that accomplishes the thing it says. "I hereby dub thee: Sir Gawain" is a sentence that actually performs an act or brings about a state of affairs by the mere fact of being uttered. Saying this phrase in the right context changes the status of something in a real way. Similarly, when I say, "I promise", or when a presiding judge speaks the words, "This court finds you guilty", these words actually perform an act; they change the status of either the relationship or the person being addressed.

So what does the fact that some words perform acts simply by being uttered have to do with consummating a marriage? Marriage is a commitment that must be enacted, and it is enacted by a certain performative utterance. Signing a document, speaking a covenant formula ("I am your husband, and you are my wife"), and sipping a cup of wine all play a role, but none of these *enact the union perfectly*. In other words, they don't embody the real essence of the union to its full.

Imagine if a group of people got together to form a theatre company. They may promise to act like a theatre company, they may sign documents stating what roles and responsibilities they commit to exercise, and they may shake hands on this agreement and even pay money for equipment, costumes, and so forth. And such actions may legally define them as a company with fiduciary obligations. But these activities don't embody in full the essence of what a theatre company is. What does do that—what consummates such a company—is actually putting on shows.

In a similar way, in ancient Israel, signing a *katubah* and sipping wine express a commitment to marry, and these acts even go so far as to form legal responsibilities. But sexual intercourse actually embodies (literally!) the essence of marital union to the full. When I think about sex in the Covenant Love Story, I therefore think about it as a performative utterance. Just as spoken utterances change one's status from *citizen* to *knight*, or *accused (or presumed innocent)* to *guilty*, so sexual intercourse in the right context enacts a marriage.

In the book of Genesis, when Jacob desired to marry Rachel but was tricked into sleeping with Leah, he was considered married to Leah due to having slept with her (Genesis 29:21-28). The completion of the sexual act is what made the marriage valid, and the legal consequences seem to have been irreversible.[89] Indeed, sexual intercourse has been considered the act which legally consummates valid marriage throughout most of history. As recently as the 2009 edition of *Black's Law Dictionary*, "consummation of marriage" is regarded as "[t]he first postmarital act of sexual intercourse between a husband and wife".[90]

The question is, *why*? What does sex say or achieve that causes it, rather than some other act, to change a couple's status from betrothed to married?

Body Language

A part of the answer has to do with the fact that covenants are family-expanding relationships, and sex is the kind of act that leads to children. Another part of the answer is that marriage calls for the commitment of one's whole self and life, and sex expresses the fullness of self-sharing. As I noted in Chapter 3 with examples of holding hands and giving flowers, many physical acts can express love. But such acts don't necessarily entail giving one's whole self (including one's potential for procreation), nor do they intrinsically call forth the sharing of all aspects of life (residence, financial destiny, etc.). The sexual act, however, is inherently oriented toward this kind of comprehensive commitment and self-gift to the other. Why? Because not only is this the social form in which love thrives, but the sharing of one's body, residence, financial destiny, and so forth is the ideal context in which to raise and nurture children, the natural fruit of the sexual act (see Chapter 5).

A third part of the answer concerns the nature of sex as *body language*. That is, sex can be a powerful form of expression or communication. It's the kind of experience through which spouses can say something to each other through their bodies. In light of the previous paragraph, what the spouses say with their bodies is, "I freely give my whole self, identity, and all aspects of my life to you forever. I make with you the kind of love that gives life to others (namely, children)". Each particular act can speak *that kind of message*, whether or not it leads to conception in a particular instance. This is another way of saying, "I freely choose to unite with you in covenant love".

Understanding sex's role in this light means viewing it as an act of the whole person—not just one aspect of him/her. A person is more than her physical organs or body parts. She is more than her reproductive potential. She is more than her capacity to experience pleasure. And she is more than her emotions and will. A person is a unity of all these, and marriage is the full union of full persons. That means that marriage is summed up or completed in an act that freely joins together in a loving gift all these dimensions of a human being. Sex has the ability to do just that—to unite these various dimensions in a performative utterance.

In other words, a fourth part of the answer for why sex is the act that consummates marriage is that sex not only conveys a message through the body but also *accomplishes* what it says in a real way. By freely intending to express a full gift of self, sex says, "full, free, fruitful, forever communion". Sex also accomplishes that kind of communion; it does so because it's the kind of act that typically forms a one-flesh union, expands families, and fosters feelings of devotion to the other.

Thus, in the Jewish Betrothal Story, the role of sex is to consummate a marriage covenant. It has the power to complete a betrothed couple's entrance into marriage because it concretely embodies the essence of the marital union. When spouses freely engage the sexual act with the intent of giving themselves fully to the other, they achieve the thing sex utters, which is a comprehensive union of persons. Sex consummates what the marriage covenant is, and each subsequent act has the power to renew that covenant. By actualising full self-giving, this act, in a very concrete and creative way, makes love.

Ethical Implications

As representatives of two stories, Mike and Chad understand sex very differently. For Mike, the purpose of sex is to have fun or perhaps express intimacy. Chad views sex as consummating and renewing a life-long commitment. Chad no doubt enjoys engaging in sex, and likely does so, in large part, because it's pleasurable, but that isn't its intrinsic purpose.[91]

What difference does this understanding make for approaching ethical questions about sex and marriage? Karin and I had already made decisions about artificial contraception and premarital sex based on other moral principles and arguments. However, viewing sex as covenant renewal provided a key to understanding Christian teaching on these and other issues on a different level.

Remember that the marriage covenant is a life-long, exclusive, family-expanding commitment. Even though modern culture's EPIC Story doesn't make sense of such requirements, they still comprise many people's vision of marriage. That is, permanence, exclusivity, and child-rearing are still part of the traditional vows said at many weddings: the officiant's words, "forsaking all others, be faithful unto her as long as you both shall live" speaks to exclusivity and life-long fidelity, and, "The union of husband and wife is intended by God ... for the procreation of children ..." calls for openness to having kids.[92]

We can conclude, then, that sexual behaviours are good and healthy if they accord with the life-long, exclusive, and procreative nature of the marriage covenant that they renew. Sexual relationships should bring the will and the body into alignment with marriage's *telos* or goal: a self-giving union of love with one other person that is faithful, fruitful, freely offered, and for the rest of life.

On these grounds:

Premarital sex is not *covenantal*—there is no publically witnessed covenant to renew, so the relationship lacks the blessings designed to flow from covenant love;

Adultery is not *faithful*—having sex with a person other than one's spouse breaks the covenant commitment to join one's identity with only that spouse for life;

Same-sex marriage is not intrinsically *fruitful*—the fact that the partners lack sexual complementarity precludes them from uniting in the kind of way that performs a single bodily function, which means they cannot consummate a family-expanding covenant;[93]

Artificial contraception is not *fruitful*—deliberately removing procreation from the sex act also precludes the formation of a one-flesh union (if the critique applies to homosexuals, it also applies to contracepting heterosexuals), so sex in this case does not renew a family-expanding covenant;[94]

Forced sex or any form of sexual violence is not *freely offered*—having non-consensual sex undermines the nature of sex as gift and dehumanises the other person by, among other things, separating their will from their body, making the essence of covenantal love—i.e., the full union of *entire* persons—impossible;[95]

No-fault divorce is not *for life*—the option to walk away from marriage without showing any wrongdoing suggests that it's a contract rather than a covenant, which is the joining of two identities "for better or worse, till death do us part";

Bigamous and polygamous sex is not *with one other person*—sex within a plural marriage breaks the covenantal commitment to give one's body, life and identity fully to only one other; thus, although not explicitly punished in the Old Testament, this practice doesn't point to Christ's relationship with his people (see next chapter);

Pornography fosters neither *self-giving to* nor *union with another person*—porn encourages viewing someone not as a person but as merely a body, its goal is self-gratification rather than self-giving, and it deliberately separates the physical pleasure of sexual arousal from the covenant union it's meant to prompt.[96]

The Jewish Betrothal Story provides us with a key lens through which to view ethical questions concerning sex and marriage. That story, however, emerged in a culture that, for many reasons, we find morally problematic today. Thus, I would not recommend embracing all its cultural elements without qualification. Nevertheless, the story's logic focuses attention on 1) the covenant nature of marriage and 2) what is entailed in consummating and renewing that covenant. In doing so, the Jewish Betrothal Story helped Karin and me think through moral issues in a practical way and reframe our notions of love, sex, and marriage.

Sensing that this story has the power to subvert the modern EPIC one, we strove to incorporate aspects of it into our wedding.

"Going to the Chapel ..."

Karin and I got married in her hometown of Salina, Kansas. The date was December 27, 1997, exactly eight months after our engagement. Several days before the big event, we had a family Christmas gathering at the house of one of Karin's relatives. Her grandfather, always cracking jokes, told her, "it's not too late to back out!"

College friends flew into town the day after Christmas, and many stayed in spare bedrooms, and even in the attic, of Karin's parents' house. I was voted by our InterVarsity group as "most likely to watch *A Few Good Men* on his wedding night". Of course, that's ridiculous—we all watched it together on the night before the wedding! After the movie, Karin and I went into a quiet room, knelt, and prayed together one last time before publicly and officially sealing the covenant of marriage. I wouldn't see her again until she walked toward me down the aisle.

Like Kayla on her big day, the next morning Karin stepped into her wedding dress and was adorned with perfume, jewels and a veil. She was then carried to the church in a ... Toyota. (But she had to submit to the normal traffic rules along the way.)

A Cup and a Bowl

For the wedding ceremony, we desired to follow our church's liturgy. Given that marriage is something bigger and older than our relationship, we didn't think we should be able to make up what it means. We wanted the church to guide us about what we were committing to rather than the other way around. We didn't write our own vows.

At the same time, though, we desired to articulate how our own story fit into a larger story of love and marriage. So we asked our pastors if it would be appropriate to tie some of the ancient Jewish betrothal and marriage customs into the ceremony. (Our pastor from Durham officiated at the ceremony, and Karin's pastor from Kansas presided over the Lord's Supper.) They both agreed with the parts we added. We put a special insert in each wedding program explaining the significance of what the congregation would see during the service. (See wedding program on pages 108-110.)

In biblical times, when the addition to the house was built and the groom went to claim his bride, he was accompanied by family and friends. I had wanted to symbolise this by having my family and a few friends stand next to me during our wedding. It's tough, though, to change too many expectations about how weddings are "supposed" to look today, so we took the more commonly accepted approach of bridesmaids on Karin's side and groomsmen on mine. I did, however, have my dad come forward and pour wine into the same cup Karin and I had used at our engagement. Again, I said, "This cup represents a covenant in blood". I handed it to her to drink, and then I did the same.

Next, we took a glass bowl and a towel and washed each other's feet. It was very special to do this while my sister sang the "Servant Song" ("... let me be as Christ to you, pray that I might have the grace to let you be my servant too. I will weep when you are weeping.

When you laugh, I'll laugh with you. I will share your joy and sorrow 'til we've seen this journey through"). The logistics, though, made washing Karin's foot more difficult than during our engagement. For one thing, she was now wearing a huge, puffy dress, which made finding her actual foot a challenge. She also wasn't sitting in a chair, but precariously standing on her left foot as I took the other for the symbolic washing. For those who might try this at their wedding, here's a helpful tip that I learned by mistake: when putting her shoe back on, remember to put the toes in first. I tried the heel-first approach several times, which didn't work. Poor Karin had to balance on one foot while all this was going on. Fortunately, her years of dancing and her natural grace kept our ceremony from becoming a viral laugh on YouTube.

Can I Get a Witness?

We performed these same acts exactly eight months earlier during our engagement. But there were several things missing that night that kept our commitment from being an official marriage. One was the presence of our pastor. Another was the public witness of the congregation. I think this witness is one of the most important but often overlooked aspects of modern wedding ceremonies.

When I am asked to give a wedding homily, I use the opportunity in part to remind the congregation how important their role is during the ceremony. When the pastor or priest asks them, "Will all of you witnessing these promises do all in your power to uphold these two persons in their marriage?" they need to think carefully about responding, "We will". They're signing up to help the couple whenever necessary in the future. That means anything from babysitting, to financial assistance, to conflict mediation—whatever the couple may require to keep their marriage strong.

Here's how I put it in a sermon at my friends Scott and Lindsay's wedding:

> The commitments made here today are not just between Scott and Lindsay, nor between them and God, but also between all of us and them and God. This was reflected moments ago when we all stood and in one voice committed to uphold and support Scott and Lindsay in their marriage. I hope you realize what this means—that today we are not just spectators and well-wishers, but members together in this newly formed covenant. You have just given these newlyweds the right and the responsibility to call upon you whenever their love proves difficult. Scott and Lindsay, when you need money, when you need resources, when you need encouragement, when you need assistance raising your 10 children (wink, wink!)—those of us in this room today are responsible for helping to meet those needs. When the rains of life start to pour down, take shelter under the roof of a church. You must call on us when you are in need, because the church as well as the world needs your marriage to be strong; we need the example of your faithfulness.

This part of the ceremony should remind us that God didn't intend couples to remain married by their own sheer effort. They require the support of others. Marriage is an institution that serves the church in very important ways (see next chapter), and the whole church has a stake in its success.

"My Body ... For You"

Karin's and my ceremony concluded with a celebration of the Lord's Supper. During this meal, we hear Christ's words, "This is my body, given for you". This intimate, bodily communion renews the new covenant that Christ inaugurated with his disciples the night before he died. The Lord's Supper is also a foretaste of this covenant's ultimate consummation at the wedding feast of the lamb (Revelation 19:9), so it's an especially appropriate event to celebrate at wedding ceremonies.

Karin and I received communion together, and then we served it to the bridal side of the congregation while our pastors served the groom's side. One of the first to come forward for communion was Karin's grandfather. He took the bread from my hand, then leaned in toward Karin's ear and whispered, "It's too late to back out now!" This 80 year-old farmer had just summed up the permanent nature of our covenant.

Both families were now free to enjoy the wedding feast.

A Larger Dance

For the reception, Karin's parents threw a Viennese Ball, or at least as close to one as you can get in the middle of Kansas. While the wedding party stayed at the church for photos, guests proceeded to the Salina Country Club for Viennese Waltz lessons.

When Karin and I got to the venue, my groomsman went ahead of us and announced our arrival by ringing a bell (we were short on shofars). We stepped out of the limousine, through the front door, and immediately onto the dance floor. We danced a solo waltz to *Blue Danube* and again experienced one of those moments where I felt I was tapping into something beautiful, ancient and solemn. As we spun around and around, I was no longer just Ryan-the-23-year-old from New Jersey, and she was no longer simply Karin-the-22-year-old from Kansas. We had stepped into larger roles and were representing larger identities: Masculine and Feminine, Call and Response, Lover and Beloved. Dance (not the freestyle gyrating that you see in modern clubs, but coordinated, partner dance) has a way of expressing the complementary and cooperative dynamic of these roles so well. What a fitting, symbolic glimpse of the two-in-one covenant we'd just entered.

As the DJ endeavoured to get more people onto the dance floor, the waltzes and polkas eventually gave way to the Macarena and the Electric Slide. These dances were individualistic and much less sophisticated, but they were at least still coordinated ... and a lot of fun. After the Hokey Pokey and the Chicken Dance, I was eager to be alone with Karin and to engage in another two-in-one dance—the consummation of the covenant!

Delayed Apocalypse[97]

One of the possible consequences of practicing natural family planning is that the wife's ovulation day could fall close to the wedding day. Sure enough, that's what happened to us. (Brides who menstruate during this time face a similar situation.) To avoid getting pregnant, we weren't able to consummate our marriage for another few days. In biblical times, Jewish couples who had already entered a covenant had to wait a long time to consummate it (as long as it took to build a house). We said we wanted our story to tie in to this larger tradition. Be careful what you wish for!

I was disappointed about the timing to say the least, but looking back, I can't help but think it turned out just right.

Leading up to our wedding, I'd heard that a woman's first sexual experience can be physically uncomfortable if not painful. In light of that, I felt that one of my goals as a husband was to make Karin feel as emotionally and psychologically comfortable as possible on that occasion. We had always taken each stage of our physical relationship slowly and one step at a time. As it turns out, we had several more stages to progress through upon getting married. Waiting patiently the first several days of our honeymoon allowed us to walk through these other stages unrushed. By the time we finally consummated our covenant—about halfway through our honeymoon—we were both less nervous and more relaxed than we would have been on our wedding night. Which means better sex!

∞

The story of entering our marriage was complete. We were grateful that the process had been full of profound beauty and significance, and that the Jewish Betrothal Story had helped unveil that for us. The really incredible thing, though, is that there's an even bigger, more beautiful, and more ancient love story that provides marriage with deeper meaning and purpose. It's time to lift the veil on that narrative.

Wedding Program Insert

The Service of Worship
Celebrating the Covenant of Marriage Between

Karin K Stoskopf
and
Ryan Scott Messmore

First Covenant Church
Salina, Kansas
December 27, 1997

In our printed wedding program, we placed an insert page (front and back) describing our understanding of the marriage covenant. We briefly told the story of the ancient Jewish betrothal process and how it illumines the larger biblical story. This helped our wedding guests to understand certain parts of our ceremony, including the sipping from the cup of wine and the foot washing.

Front

Dear Friends,

We understand our wedding ceremony to be a service of worship in the church. It is here, among the members of our Christian community, that we make public our covenant to live the rest of our lives as husband and wife. We enter this marriage covenant for the mutual edification and upbuilding of each other and the church, for the procreation and nurture of children, and for the witness to the world of Christ's faithful, self-giving relationship with his people. Therefore, it is appropriate that we gather together in the name of Christ, where he himself is present, to declare our wedding vows and to have them witnessed by the people who belong to him.

Following the declaration of the intentions of our covenant and the 'giving of the bride' by her father, we will sip from a cup. We do this in accordance with the ancient Jewish tradition of two families establishing the terms of marriage between their children and then sealing that covenant with a cup of wine. As a symbol of the covenant, the father of the young man would pour a cup of wine and hand it to his son, who would turn to the young woman and say, "This cup represents a new covenant in blood." (Covenants in Biblical times were sealed with blood; see Hebrews 9:16-22.) The couple would not drink from the same cup again until their wedding day.

After sealing the covenant, the young man would return to his father's home and build a room for his bride onto the side of the house. The house, called an 'insula,' would continue to expand throughout the years with new additions as each son in the family got married. The bride-to-be did not know when the young man would come back to claim her as his bride, so she had to be ready for his arrival at all times. During this betrothal period, she was not to be seen by the groom until their wedding day. Therefore, when she would enter a public area where she might encounter him, she would wear a veil over her face. When the husband-to-be completed the addition onto his father's insula, he would return with his family and friends to the home of the young woman and claim her as his bride.

Christ build on this tradition in his word and action during the 'Last Supper.' On that night, Christ took a cup, gave it to his disciples and said, "This cup is the new covenant in my blood" (Luke 22:20). After his disciples drank from the cup, Jesus declared, "I will not drink of this fruit of the vine from now on until that day when I drink it anew with you in my Father's kingdom" (Matt. 27:29). During the communion meal, Christ showed his love for his disciples by washing their feet (John 13:5). Shortly thereafter he gave himself up to be crucified, and in so doing the brideprice of the new covenant was paid. John 14:2-3 tells us that Christ is now at his Father's house preparing a room for us, and that he will one day come back and take us to be with him as his bride. Indeed, Jesus describes the kingdom of heaven as a wedding banquet in Matt. 22:2, and John describes the 'wedding supper of the Lamb' in his revelation of the end of time (Revelation 19).

In light of the way in which the ancient Jewish wedding tradition illuminates the covenant nature of marriage, we have sought to embody that tradition in our courtship and betrothal, as well as in today's service. Upon securing the consent of Karin's parents, we were betrothed to one another on April 27, 1997 on top of the Duke Chapel Tower. On that rainy night, we sipped from the same cup that will be used in the service today, and, following Christ's example, we washed one another's feet as a symbol of our commitment to love and serve one another for life. We have not drunk from this cup since that night, nor will Karin's veil be lifted during today's service until the declaration of marriage. Although we enacted these rituals and declared our promises to each other on April 27, we recognized that we were not yet married in the eyes of the church. This demonstrates how essential the public witness of our vows by the Christian community is to the meaning of marriage. It is your witness and support which make our already-stated promises marriage. Today we agree to make our relationship accountable to you, the church, realizing that we need you to help us love each other well. For those of you who do not consider yourselves members of the Christian community, we hope today both to demonstrate the joy of being in the body of Christ and to mirror the kind of relationship he has with us. We pray that we may all drink anew together of the fruit of the vine with him at the eternal wedding banquet!

Our Wedding

Borrowing from the ancient Jewish tradition, we sealed our marriage covenant by sipping wine from the same cup we used at our engagement. Also during the wedding ceremony, we washed each other's feet (photos on the following page), imitating Christ's self-giving love on the night he established the New Covenant with his disciples.

7

THE (EVEN) LARGER LOVE STORY

The tale told so far—of desiring intimate, bodily communion, entering the process of covenant making, preparing for its faithful fulfilment, and celebrating its consummation—is significant because it follows the contours of a much deeper, ancient narrative: God's history with His creation. The Covenant Love story provides the narrative structure for Scripture; its plot involves the loving Creator pursuing an intimate, family-expanding relationship with His beloved people.

In other words, from the first chapter to the last, the form of the Bible's underlying story is that of a marriage. Indeed, the reason we paid attention to Chad and Kayla's betrothal and wedding tradition is because it helped illumine significant aspects of this Grand Love Story.[98]

Scripture's Story of Covenant Love

Discerning the marital shape of salvation history requires attending to the events whereby God enters, seals, renews, expands and remains faithful to His family-forming covenant with Israel and the church. What follows is a very brief synopsis of that story.

Holy Couple - In the opening chapter of Genesis, God creates the first humans: "in the image of God he created them; male and female he created them" (Genesis 1:27). God told them to "be fruitful and increase in number", and they united to each other and became "one flesh" (Genesis 2:24).

Holy Family - Adam and Eve, representing all of humanity, disobeyed God and were exiled from the Garden of Eden. Things only unravelled from there. Ten generations later, when the human heart became too corrupt, God—Yahweh in the Old Testament—sent a great flood. But to Noah and his family, whom He saved through the ark, Yahweh said, "Be fruitful and increase in number and fill the earth. ... I now establish my covenant with you and with your descendants after you" (Genesis 9:1, 9). Like Adam, however, Noah soon broke his covenant with Yahweh.

Holy Tribe - Not willing to abandon His promise, God, after another ten generations, formed a covenant with Abram. This was the kind of covenant that makes its members part of the same family. To ratify this covenant, Yahweh had Abram cut in half a heifer, a goat, and a ram; then, in a dream, Abram saw a smoking firepot with a blazing torch pass between the carcasses (Genesis 15:9-17). Abram, though, doubted that Yahweh would fulfil his promise to give him numerous descendants, so Yahweh re-established the covenant. This time, Abram had to seal his special relationship by cutting himself in the rite of circumcision.[99] In this covenant, Yahweh gave him a new name (Abraham) and promised to bless all nations on earth through his offspring (Genesis 17:5; 22:18).

Holy Nation - A few hundred years later, Abraham's descendants worshipped pagan gods in Egypt, where they would become slaves. To fulfil His covenant with Abraham, Yahweh acted in a definitive way to free these Israelites and prepare a home for them: a land in which Yahweh would dwell together with His beloved people. After rescuing her out of bondage in Egypt and across the Red Sea, Yahweh established a covenant with Israel at Mt. Sinai. In covenant-forming language He declared to Moses, "I will look on you with favor and make you fruitful and increase your numbers, and I will keep my covenant with you. ... I will put my dwelling place among you ... I will walk among you and be your God, and you will be my people" (Leviticus 26:9, 11-12). Yahweh also gave His covenant partner a valuable gift: the Law. Moses sealed the covenant by saying, "This is the blood of the covenant" and sprinkling it on the altar as well as the people (Exodus 24:6, 8). The Passover meal would be the regular means of commemorating Israel's rescue and renewing her covenant with Yahweh (Exodus 12:14).

Holy Kingdom - The nation of Israel became a kingdom several hundred years later. Yahweh covenanted with David to establish the throne of his kingdom forever and to build a house (temple) in which Yahweh would dwell with Israel undisturbed (2 Samuel 7:8-16).

Israel's identity was to be forever tied to this family-forming covenant relationship, which the Old Testament prophets spoke of in marital terms. "For your Maker is your husband—the LORD Almighty is his name", proclaimed Isaiah (Isaiah 54:5). Ezekiel recounts Yahweh declaring to Israel:

> I gave you my solemn oath and entered into a covenant with you ... and you became mine. I bathed you with water and washed the blood from you and put ointments on you. I clothed you with an embroidered dress and put sandals of fine leather on you. I dressed you in fine linen and covered you with costly garments. I adorned you with jewelry: I put bracelets on your arms and a necklace around your neck, and I put a ring on your nose, earrings on your ears and a beautiful crown on your head (Ezekiel 16:8b-12).[100]

This spousal relationship was intended to be fruitful; the blessings that would flow from Israel's covenant were meant for the whole world. According to Yahweh, "It is too small a thing for you to be my servant to restore the tribes of Jacob and bring back those of Israel I have kept; I will also make you a light for the Gentiles, that my salvation may reach to the ends of the earth" (Isaiah 49:6).[101]

Throughout the Old Testament, however, Israel continued to act unfaithfully, failing to be the light to the nations Yahweh called her to be. Rather than focusing outward to multiply God's love, Israel viewed the covenant blessings as intended for her alone. Moreover, she worshipped other gods, which Hosea, Isaiah, and Jeremiah likened to adultery. "'But like a woman unfaithful to her husband, so you, Israel, have been unfaithful to me,' declares the LORD" (Jeremiah 3:20).[102] The prophets spoke of God's reaction in terms of the anger of a jealous husband. Again, Ezekiel's imagery is especially striking:

> You engaged in prostitution with the Egyptians, your neighbors with large genitals, and aroused my anger with your increasing promiscuity. ... You engaged in prostitution with the Assyrians too, because you were insatiable; and even after that, you still were not satisfied. Then you increased your promiscuity to include Babylonia, a land of merchants, but even with this you were not satisfied. I am filled with fury against you ... You adulterous wife! You prefer strangers to your own husband! ... you have despised my oath by breaking the covenant (Ezekiel 16:26, 28-30, 32, 59).

Despite this anger and jealousy, Yahweh remained faithful, promising to rescue Israel from her adulterous ways, restore her purity, and dwell with her once more. For example, Yahweh commanded Hosea to demonstrate His reconciling relationship with unfaithful Israel: "Go, show your love to your wife again, though she is loved by another man and is an adulteress. Love her as the LORD loves the Israelites, though they turn to other gods" (Hosea

3:1). Moreover, Yahweh promised to send an anointed servant in the future who, like a groom, would come to claim her as his own and take her home: "I will make a new covenant with the people of Israel and with the people of Judah. ... I will be their God, and they will be my people" (Jeremiah 31:31, 33).[103]

Jesus Christ: The Groom - This anticipated groom was born in a manger to a Jewish girl named Mary, who was betrothed but had not consummated her marriage; she was therefore a virgin but legally bound to her husband, Joseph (Luke 2:5; Matthew 1:18-20). Shortly after his birth, Magi from the East brought him gifts that a groom would have worn: gold, frankincense, and myrrh. In the Gospel of Mark, Jesus refers to himself as "the bridegroom" (Mark 2:19). Jesus' cousin, John the Baptist, described himself as "the friend of the bridegroom" (John 3:29) and called people to undergo baptism as a ritual bath representing spiritual cleansing.

Jesus performed his first public miracle at a wedding in Cana, where he turned water into wine; in doing so, he fulfilled the role of a Jewish groom, whose responsibility it was to provide wine for his guests (John 2:1-11). Furthermore, as Abraham's servant had asked Rebekah for water at a well many years earlier, Jesus engaged in a similar conversation with a Samaritan woman at a well (see John 4:3-26). (In this betrothal-initiating encounter, he indicated that God desired to wed himself not only to Israel but to non-Jewish believers in Yahweh as well.[104])

And remember that, when a typical Jewish man who was betrothed was asked, "When is your wedding date?" he would respond, "Only my father knows". When Jesus' disciples asked when he would come at the end of the age, Jesus responded, "But about that day or hour no one knows, not even the angels in heaven, nor the Son, but only the Father" (Matthew 24:36). He then told them to keep watch because on that day there will be people who are like virgins going out to meet the groom's procession back to the father's house, but who do not bring enough oil for their lamps, and therefore are not allowed entrance (Matthew 25:1-13).

When celebrating his final Passover meal, Jesus, the Son of God, established the new covenant that the prophets had foretold. Remember that, upon articulating the conditions of the marriage covenant in a *katubah* and sealing a betrothal with a cup of wine (the same cup that would be used at his wedding), a typical Jewish man would return to his father's house to build a room for his bride. We can discern in Jesus' words and actions during the Last Supper some intriguing echoes of this process. On that night, he poured water into a basin and gave his disciples' feet a bath. He then articulated the conditions of the covenant: "A new command I give you: Love one another. As I have loved you, so you must love one another. ... Greater love has no one than this: to lay down one's life for one's friends" (John 13:34-35, 15:13). He also handed them a cup of wine and said, "This cup is the new covenant in my blood" (1 Corinthians 11:25).

His next words were, "I tell you, I will not drink from this fruit of the vine from now on until that day when I drink it new with you in my Father's kingdom" (Matthew 26:29). Moreover, Jesus tells them that he will soon depart from them to go to his Father's house: "And if I go and prepare a place for you, I will come back and take you to be with me" (John 14:3). The bridechamber, a room typically designed according to the measurements and decor of the holy of holies, would be prepared by Jesus the High Priest for God's eternal union with His people.

The next day, Jesus, dressed in a seamless tunic and wearing a crown upon his head, shed his own blood on the cross. This was the ultimate act of self-giving love for his people. Upon taking a sip of wine from a sponge, he completed the Passover meal (which had been left unfinished the night before) and uttered his final words, "It is consummated".[105] Having concluded the Passover, as well as an entire life of faithfulness, Jesus not only renewed but also perfectly fulfilled the covenant.

Holy Church - Finally, like grooms of his day, Jesus gave his new bride several gifts. He commissioned baptism as a way of entering into his own family—the body of Christ. (Some traditions have actually referred to baptism as a nuptial bath.) He established the practice of communion or the Eucharist as a regular renewal of the new covenant. After his resurrection and before his ascension, he also presented his bride with the gift of the Holy Spirit (John 20:22).

Yahweh had promised to pour out the Spirit upon Israel if she exercised faithfulness to the covenant. Jesus fulfilled this covenant faithfulness on her behalf, so she received the Spirit as a gift and a covenant blessing. In the time before Jesus' return, the Holy Spirit prepares and equips his bride for the ultimate wedding day. This includes guiding and assisting her to grow in faithfulness to God and continue the outward-focused mission of extending His love to the world. The Spirit animates and empowers the members of Christ's family for sacrificial love, which is another way of saying that the Spirit gives life—the body of Christ is spiritually fruitful.

In the meantime, the church keeps watch for the great Apocalypse: the great *unveiling* of "a new heaven and a new earth" (Isaiah 65:17 and Revelation 21:1). According to the book of Revelation, Christ will return to claim the church as his bride. His coming will be announced by the blowing of trumpets, and his people will shout:

> "Let us rejoice and be glad
> and give him glory!
> For the wedding of the Lamb has come,

and his bride has made herself ready.

Fine linen, bright and clean,

was given her to wear" (Revelation 19:7-8).

The final chapter of the Bible describes this day as the appearance of "the new Jerusalem ... prepared as a bride beautifully dressed for her husband. ... God's dwelling place is now among the people, and he will dwell with them. They will be his people, and God himself will be with them and be their God" (Revelation 21:2-3). On that day, the bride will be at home with the Son and in perfect communion with the Father; she will achieve a one-flesh union with God in his consummated Kingdom.

"Blessed are those who are invited to the wedding supper of the Lamb!" (Revelation 19:9).

A Growing Family

Scripture provides a narrative about a grand marriage. Husband and wife imagery—i.e., two uniting as one—doesn't just appear here and there in a couple of verses. Instead, as New Testament scholar N. T. Wright observes, the Bible is "an entire narrative which works with this complementarity so that a male-plus-female marriage is a signpost or a signal about the goodness of the original creation and God's intention for the eventual new heavens and new earth".[106]

This is a story of a Lover who seeks out bodily, covenant union with His beloved. The Creator of the universe enters a covenant with His creation; God binds His identity to a people and ours to Him. The triune God opens His divine family and extends His kinship relations to us. This means that His people receive from God the personal care and protection of a dad for his children. He promises to provide, guide, and nourish as a proud papa does. It also means that the church, in her union with Christ, will receive the same inheritance that Jesus the divine Son receives. What is that inheritance? Nothing less than the entire life and love of the Father. That's really good news!

In short, the events of Scripture, culminating in the Incarnation, Crucifixion, Resurrection, and Ascension, are acts through which God says to Israel and the church, "I give my whole self, identity, and all aspects of my life to you forever".

It is important to note how God's covenant with Israel was a family-expanding relationship. As we've seen, Yahweh established various covenants in the Old Testament. These did not nullify or replace the covenants that came before; rather, each one expanded the scope of God's people: The covenant with Adam included a *marriage* of two people, which was expanded to a *household* in the covenant with Noah, to a *tribe* in the covenant with Abraham, to a *nation* in the covenant with Moses, and to a *national kingdom* in the covenant with David. Each covenant extends God's kinship relations, and, thus, His promised blessings, to a wider circle of members. The new covenant established by Jesus does this as well, inviting not only Jews but also Gentiles—indeed, people from every nation, language, and ethnicity—into God's family.[107]

God's covenant with His people therefore has broader purposes than their own happiness and well-being. It is not meant for them alone; it is meant to be outward-focused. God covenants with one—and only one—people as the chosen means by which to offer a relationship to others.[108] His method is to commit to a family and then to expand that family by bringing others in. The widening of God's family—the sharing of divine communion—is the overall goal toward which the biblical story moves. God invites us to become His adopted children by becoming the bride of His Son!

Living in Light of the Larger Story

The nature of God's covenant with Israel reinforces a very important truth about earthly marriages: they have a purpose beyond the spouses' happiness. Marriage is a calling that serves a larger social function. What is that function? First, marriage is oriented towards children, and thus anchors the context in which healthy citizens are born, nurtured, protected, educated and raised. As I noted in Chapter 5, the state has a vested interest in promoting marriage for this reason. But having children is a function that serves not just the state but also the church.

In a world in which many young people think, "I wouldn't want a child to have to experience this degree of dysfunctional mess",[109] the church continues to hope. In confessing God as an "Almighty Father", the church claims that God rules his good creation lovingly and parentally. Thus, as Hauerwas argues, having children is one way the church witnesses to this hope in God's providential care.[110] To get married is therefore to enlist in, or at least to be open to, this parental responsibility that serves the common good.

In addition to producing and raising children, spouses are called to serve another significant social function. In a cynical world in which people say, "Trust nobody; everyone will let you down eventually, so look out for number one", the church continues to speak of unconditional, sacrificial faithfulness to an other. She asserts that the Creator of all things has committed to love her, no matter what. He will remain faithful and will not abandon His people, come what may. That's quite a claim. How would the world ever begin to believe it? How would our culture even know that this kind of persevering, covenant love is possible, let alone become attracted to it? The answer: by observing faithful marriages.

Two people committing exclusively to each other forever, with a fruitful love that pours itself out for others, testifies to a deep reality. St. Paul says that it points to the relationship that Christ has with the church (Ephesians 5:25-33). The *life-long* commitment of marriage mirrors God's undying faithfulness to His covenant; the *exclusiveness* of marriage witnesses to God's singular election of Israel and the church; and the *orientation to children* of sex and marriage points to the family-expanding fruitfulness of God's outward-focused mission.

Our marriages can also show the world that covenant unions are not based on felt love. By sticking together through rough times, we witness to the active love of God, who continues to give Himself to the church, not because He continues to like her, but because He exercises covenant faithfulness. As any husband and wife grow older together, they will inevitably disappoint and fail each other; they will see each other's inner imperfections highlighted and outer beauty succumb to time and gravity. This need not cause fear or uncertainty, as long as their marriage is grounded in something deeper: covenant faithfulness. Without the concrete embodiment of God's self-giving love called marriage, the world might remain in doubt that this sort of commitment is possible.

Thus, marriage—and sex, which consummates and renews it—is serious business. Karin and I said we wanted to understand these realities in a more healthy, hopeful and perhaps even holy manner. As it turns out, there really is a way to do that! Our sexuality bears the blueprint of God's plan to enter into a family-expanding covenant with His people. It also echoes the very life of the Trinity, in which three become one through life-giving self-donation.

Sex, therefore, isn't a recreational sport to enter into lightly. And marriage isn't simply a private relationship you enjoy with your "number one" soul mate, let alone the kind of spur-of-the-moment brainstorm that Bruno Mars sings about: "We're looking for something dumb to do / Hey, baby, I think I wanna marry you!

… If we wake up and you want to break up, that's cool / No I won't blame you; it was fun, girl". Rather, marriage is a sacred summons to undergo intentional preparations, take on significant responsibilities, and make considerable sacrifices. By the same token, a wedding isn't just a celebration of intimacy but a commissioning for a monumental mission on behalf of the church for the world. Within this context, sex and marriage come with tremendous blessings.

To sum this all up, God has invited husbands and wives *in* to something larger than themselves. Our marriages find their true fulfilment *in* the context of Christ's union with the church. Our story finds its true direction *in* His story. Our love thrives most when it participates *in* the divine nature[111]—when we live and move and have our being *in* Love Himself.

EPILOGUE
After the Honeymoon

In the 19 years since Karin and I were married, the EPIC Story has only become more dominant and audacious in Western culture. Today social media makes it much easier to identify and indulge people who view sex simply as erotic sport. In particular, no-strings sex apps foster what some social commentators call "the jump-cut phenomenon". Referring to the jump-cut edit in a pornographic movie, many approach online dates expecting "Hawaiian pizza in one scene ... a sexual frenzy in the next".[112] It's assumed that this is just the way life works—minimal conversation, minimal connection, just a quick score on a Friday night.

Recently, Karin and I tried out a new hibachi/teppanyaki restaurant. While we were waiting for our table to be prepared, we enjoyed people watching at the bar. A young, handsome man wrapped his arm around the waist of a very attractive young woman who was dressed in a tight-fitting, revealing outfit. When the man went to get drinks, she talked with an older gentleman, who we assumed was the young man's father. Perhaps the man had arranged this occasion to introduce his girlfriend to his dad, we figured. Wow, were we wrong.

We ended up sitting next to them around the tableside grill. Before the chef could build a fire-erupting volcano out of onion rings, things got very awkward. The young man said something to the young lady that made her almost erupt. Red-faced and quite upset, she stomped out of the restaurant. When the young man ran after her, the older gentleman casually informed us that she'd rejected their proposal for that evening. They were gay partners seeking a threesome with a young female. She, on the other hand, had expected to hook up only with the younger man, whom she had met online and thought was straight. Karin and I spent the rest of dinner getting to know the story of the older gentleman (it wasn't quite the three-way exchange he had anticipated) and pondering the brave new technosexual age in which we live.

Challenges Endured

It's an age of seeking, celebrating, experimenting with, and protecting individual identity. Ours is an era of overthrowing traditional assumptions and overcoming bodily and sexual limitations, so that everyone's free to be the character they prefer in a story they write themselves. Sadly, many people don't realise that, rather than living as an autonomous author, they're actually following the script of a dominant story they've given authority to unawares.

In this cultural moment, Karin and I continue to be thankful that we've submitted to a different story. In the Covenant Love Story, the built-in meaning and limits of bodies and sex are not shunned but embraced, and identities are not created and guarded but (to a certain extent) received, grown into, and shared. We've chosen to follow this script because we think it's more beautiful, true, and freeing than any other on offer.

In almost two decades of marriage, Karin and I have had to rely many times on the Covenant Love Story and its Author to help us sustain our covenant. When I pursued my doctoral studies at Oxford, Karin and our two boys remained back in the U.S. We were once again faced with a gruelling, long-distance relationship for painful stretches of time; we once again had to call upon the patience, self-control, and commitment to active love that we'd cultivated in college.

Shortly thereafter, our family was called to Australia so I could lead a liberal arts college (tertiary level). Leaving a familiar network of support and starting over in a new country has been very difficult at times. Karin, especially, has had to give herself for a larger good than her own comfort, which the Covenant Love Story helped train her to do with much grace.

Nothing, though, challenged us like August and September of 2001.

With great excitement, we went to see the doctor for the first sonogram of our first pregnancy. Afterwards we intended to go out to lunch to celebrate the fruitfulness of our marriage. Upon arriving in the office, the doctor spread gel on Karin's stomach, positioned the instrument in place, and brought up a fuzzy image on the computer screen. Now was the moment we would meet our baby for the first time!

But nothing happened.

The doctor paused. The screen was still. Why couldn't we see any movement? Why couldn't we hear anything? Where was the heartbeat? What was wrong? Please ... No!

The doctor then spoke the dark, cold word: miscarriage.

She left the room so Karin and I could process the news alone. It was the most empty, lifeless, crippling moment of my life. We willed ourselves out to the parking garage of the hospital, but we couldn't make it any further. With our backs against the harsh concrete wall of the parking building, we sat and wept. Nobody had prepared us for this. We had never heard miscarriage discussed among our friends or family or at our church.

Shortly thereafter the tragic events of September 11 occurred. As I watched the television footage that followed the collapse of the World Trade Center, I saw numerous people hold up photos of missing loved ones. Even after a week had gone by and it became clear that no more survivors would be found, victims' families still held up their photos to the TV cameras and the world. I felt as if I knew why. In time, Karin and I expected that our hearts would be able to move on past the miscarriage, but in a strange way I didn't want that to happen yet. That would mean that this human being that we never had a chance to talk to would be forgotten—there was a little life who deserved to be known, but wouldn't. I found myself wanting to hold up the sonogram to the world so this tiny person would be remembered.

In time, Karin and I did move on, and we got pregnant again. But then we lost our second pregnancy to another miscarriage. Again, we were devastated. And this time we began to face the possibility that we might not be able (biologically) to have kids. We hadn't considered this when thinking about the Covenant Love Story; given the importance of marriage being family-expanding and fruitful—and of sexuality being naturally oriented toward procreation—this really threw us. How would we think of our marriage? How would this affect our relationship?

I really wanted to be a dad, and such a situation might tempt one to leave and find another partner with whom to have kids. But that wasn't a temptation for me. At that moment, there was no question in either of our minds that, whatever the future held, we would face it together. I had joined my identity to Karin's, and our destiny would be a shared destiny, for better or worse. Thanks to the Covenant Love Story, we were able to see that our marriage could bear fruit in ways beyond giving birth to our kids: among other things, we were called to show the world the kind of covenant faithfulness that God exercises towards us.

Lessons Learned

Thankfully, God did bless us with three successful pregnancies and three happy, healthy kids (and one of them really did lose his shoe in a soccer game while running for the ball). In 2012, 15 years after Karin and I were engaged and married, we took Joshua, Christopher, and Katie to Duke to share with them a bit of our story. (See photo, page 72.) When it comes to introducing them to the Jewish Betrothal Story and the countercultural lessons we gleaned from it, here are the primary points we hope they'll take away:

➤ Love is an action, not just a felt attraction.

➤ Romantic and sexual desires are healthy promptings toward personal communion. *Eros* is meant to serve *agape*. The problem comes when we separate the former from the latter and seek physical gratification as an end in itself.

➤ The basis of marriage is not intimate feelings but covenant faithfulness.

➤ The purposes of sex include procreation, uniting a couple in love, and consummating and renewing marriage. Sex is intended to be covenant renewal.

➤ Marriage, sex, and procreation have a built-in connection; they tend to flourish when pursued together.

My hope in writing this book is that you, too, will reflect deeply on these claims. May I encourage you also to consider how these convictions can lead to, and emerge from, regular, concrete practices? We live in a larger cultural context that forms and shapes us at a subconscious level. It's not enough to try to counter this influence with simply a theory—even a correct theory—about sexuality. Instead, what's needed is a *way of life*, supported by a *surrounding culture* that encourages *formative habits* through *routine, ritual actions*.[113] Some of the actions and habits I suggest include:

➤ cultivating self-control through spiritual disciplines (like fasting, financial giving, and so forth);

➤ seeking third-party input into your relationships (from parents, pastors and other people who know you well);

➤ speaking of love as a verb—i.e., trying not to use phrases like "fall in love" and "love at first sight";

➤ moving slowly and patiently through the early stages of your physical relationship;

➤ writing down specific acts of love to commit to as you near engagement;

➤ discussing marriage expectations in detail *before* getting engaged, perhaps through pre-engagement counselling;

➤ taking intentional steps to prepare for marriage, like budgeting and attending parenting classes;

➤ learning ovulation signs before entering a sexual relationship; and

➤ inserting into your proposal and wedding some gestures that capture their larger meaning, while still submitting to the authority of your church's traditional vows and practices.[114]

A Wave of Gratitude

Even though marriage is intended to bear deep meaning and profound beauty, and to be renewed regularly through pleasurable sex, reality on the ground can look much different. It's not pure "happily ever after" bliss.

Despite the intentionality that Karin and I invested in our engagement and marriage, we find that living as husband and wife poses many daily challenges. For every big challenge that comes our way (like an international move or a miscarriage), there are a thousand little ones. Each of them tempts us to focus inwardly on ourselves and to please our own bodily desires rather than to sacrifice for a larger good. The fabric of a marriage, however, is woven by all of the seemingly small gestures, words, actions, and reactions that we make about where to direct our attention and love. This was captured in an incident that occurred while writing the original draft of this book.

In July 2011, my church small group took a trip to Ocean City, Maryland. One of the other dads and I were casually talking while in the ocean, when I turned to see a 10-foot wave careening toward us. My friend said, "Oh, you've got to take that one!" I wasn't in the right position to catch it, but I lay down on my boogie board and turned toward the shore. The next thing I was aware of was extreme pain in my face and back. The crest of the wave came down directly on my head, slamming it into the ocean floor.

Everything went blurry. Caught in a washing machine-like vortex of water, I struggled to remain conscious. All of my effort went into getting out of the water before I blacked out.

As I limped into bed that evening, my lower back and my left wrist were very sore, my head was pounding, and I felt stinging pinpricks under my eyes. I must have inhaled a good dose of the ocean during the accident, and each time I turned my head on my pillow, the water resituated itself amidst my swollen sinus cavities. To make things worse, our two-year-old, Katie, was sleeping right next to me. (We don't usually do this, but with 15 people in a small beach house, we had to squeeze six bodies into our room—three boys on the floor and Karin, Katie, and me in the bed.) I'm not sure how a 20-pound (or 9 kg) girl manages to confiscate 80 percent of the mattress, but Katie ended up sprawling diagonally across the bed with her heels driving into my lower back.

This was awful! Time crawled at a dreadfully cruel pace. I began to feel very sorry for myself, and my tossing and turning woke Karin up. After hearing of my agony, she transitioned Katie onto the floor, got me a drink of water, and propped up some pillows in the bed for me to lie on. I asked if she would hold my hand for a couple minutes, and she willingly did so, even though it meant lying on the opposite side than the one she usually sleeps on. After realising this, I let go and told her she could turn over and go back to sleep. She whispered, "It's okay. I'm happy to continue holding your hand if it makes you feel better".

That's when it hit me. Karin was offering me her body as a gift.

Finding Myself in Love

It was a small gesture, but many small gestures combine to form habits, habits combine to form character, and character can shape the destiny of a marriage.

Earlier that very day, as we were driving to Ocean City, I had read several entries in John Paul II's *Theology of the Body*. He spoke about the "meaning of the body" in terms of its ability to facilitate the "gifting" of oneself to one's spouse. Reading it, I remember thinking, "This sounds really attractive as a theory, but it seems so distant to the meaning and motivation of sex as couples actually experience it today". Little did I realise that that very night I would catch a deeper glimpse into the author's profound insight.

My body isn't meant for providing me pleasure as much as it is meant to enable me to give myself to others as a gift. And yet, after 19 years of marriage, how often I forget that! Just a couple days before our beach trip, I had complained to Karin that our sex drives weren't firing on the same levels. Then, the night of the accident, I was feeling sorry and even angry about the pain in my bones, muscles, and sinews. My body, meant for giving myself away, too often becomes the object of self-focus and attention.

As I thought about that, I realised that the pain in my head was the kind of pain Karin describes when experiencing migraines. Except whereas I was being thrown by one headache, Karin is tormented by migraines several times a month. I also remembered that Karin's headaches often cause pain in her shoulders and lower back. I was getting a one-time taste of what my wife suffers on a regular basis. But when she's in pain, my response is more often annoyance than sympathy, let alone self-giving. Yet here was Karin, woken up in the middle of the night after a tiring day, and her response was to give her body—her very self—to me as a gift.

Needless to say, we didn't have sex right then and there. But at 3:00 a.m. in Ocean City I was reminded of the kind of generous, sacrificial relationship that sex is meant to embody.

Even after years and years of thinking about and training for the self-gifting that marriage requires, that sort of response doesn't come easily for me. Christian discipleship—learning to love others as Christ loves us—is an ongoing process. I've got a long way to go in this department, but it helps to know that the journey fits into a much larger story. The transcendent power that animates our lives and our marriage is the same power that moves the sun and the stars. As Karin and I daily struggle to serve each other with our bodies, to become gifts for the other, we are going "with the grain" of the triune God.

I couldn't ask for a better partner on this journey of becoming more like Christ and learning to *participate in* his relationship to the Father. Karin has helped me to *take part in* the self-gift that constitutes the very nature of the Trinity.

I think I'm *in* Love!

AFTERWORD
Feeling This Story Isn't For You?

Whether it's cultivating self-control when dating or exercising faithfulness in marriage, Covenant Love Story relationships take practice and hard work. That's one reason why people may decide this story isn't for them. Another reason might have to do with the fact that we all struggle with the purity and permanent commitment that characterise this story's ideal. Real life just seems too messy and complicated. How could we possibly hold ourselves and our relationships to such a standard?

Here it's important to remember the Grand Love Story that the Covenant Love Story reflects: the story of a God of grace who not only calls us to the good but also empowers us by His Spirit with what's needed to achieve it. That includes a way back (forgiveness) when we stumble. That also includes a community (the body of Christ) to help us.

In a broken world, sexuality and romantic relationships can be breeding grounds for pain and brokenness. As we seek to live in alignment with the biblical story, we will all find ourselves with crosses to bear: struggling not to go too far physically on a date; resisting the temptation to indulge in free, easily accessible porn; managing a perceived mismatch between one's experience of gender and biological sex; remaining faithful in marriage after falling out of infatuation; dealing with infertility; grappling with same-sex attraction; giving up sex for blocks of time when practicing NFP;

navigating loneliness and abstinence after divorce; and carrying guilt or disappointment related to any of the contexts above and countless others.

The church is a community of people struggling to carry all sorts of crosses relating to sexuality and marriage. Rather than demonising any single situation and ignoring the others, we need to acknowledge that our shared, fallen nature causes us all to struggle in different ways. We need to help each other—through encouraging, convicting, listening, learning, serving, sharing, teaching, and providing accountability and resources—as we together strive to live more in line with God's call.[115]

Some Particular Struggles

For those who may regret prior sexual decisions, remember the history of Old Testament Israel. She indulged in promiscuous behaviour and committed adultery, which disappointed and angered the Lord greatly. Yet He is a God of love who never gives up on His beloved. The same God who continued to rescue Israel back into communion with Himself continues to offer forgiveness and restoration to you. He offers it to all of us. We are never too dirty or broken to be denied God's reconciliation; we simply need to confess our failings, accept Christ's forgiveness, and commit to bathing in His waters and preparing ourselves for His wedding table. Regardless of the past, Christ is able to make his bride spotless, if we are willing to sip from the covenant cup he offers.

For those who may dabble or dwell in pornography, you know this is a very difficult, ongoing battle. It's tempting to believe that you're too far in—too addicted—to bring this area of your life before God. But His reconciling and liberating grace is for you, too.

It's also tempting to justify viewing porn, even if you look "only occasionally", by thinking that nobody's really getting harmed. My encouragement is to keep reminding yourself that porn isn't neutral in its effects. Far from it. Viewing porn releases addiction-causing chemicals that desensitise the brain to the same stimulus over time (requiring more explicit images and content to achieve the same level of arousal). Porn also creates unrealistic expectations for sex and can hinder emotional intimacy with a real human being. And it leads to treating those who prompt sexual desires within us as pleasure objects rather than as persons. This encourages a mentality of self-gratification rather than self-giving. Thus, when sexually-loaded images show up in the mind's living room asking for hospitality, it's best to show them immediately to the door. If you value true freedom, place whatever obstacles you need to help steer clear of likely encounters with porn. Resistance may seem futile, but the short-term pleasure isn't worth the long-term enslavement, nor the inability to enjoy really good sex in a marriage. Keep battling.

For those who struggle with singleness, the church needs to hear from you. Especially in Christian social contexts, singles can too often be made to feel like they don't belong. What's more, the positive good that Christians rightly highlight about marriage can make it seem as if one can't be happy, or within God's will, outside of matrimony. That's simply not true, and it makes an idol out of marriage. God's covenant union with His people includes both marrieds and singles, and the fruitful love we're called to offer in response takes many forms (not just begetting offspring).[116]

Furthermore, just as married couples are called to point to God and His plan in a certain way, so too are singles. Whether we realise it or not, singles have a valuable service to offer the church and the watching world: they testify that God's Kingdom depends not on heirs but conversion. They bear testimony that "our future is not guaranteed by the family but by God".[117] Moreover, as theological ethicist Oliver O'Donovan has written, the early church:

> conceived of marriage and singleness as alternative vocations, each a worthy form of life, the two together comprising the whole Christian witness to the nature of the affectionate community. The one declared that God had vindicated the order of creation, the other pointed beyond it to its eschatological transformation.[118]

The "eschatological" consummation of creation that O'Donovan refers to—that is, the future Kingdom of God in its full perfection—is described by Jesus as a time in which "people will neither marry nor be given in marriage" (Matthew 22:30). At that time, our primary marital union will be with Christ.[119] For this reason, some religious traditions call for their leaders to practice celibacy—not because sex is bad, but because these leaders testify to a marriage with a heavenly spouse. They show the church and the world a preview of the coming spousal union with God.

But not only priests feel called to practice celibacy; some lay people do as well. One Christian author recently wrote about a friend who asked his church for a liturgy in which he could take a public vow of celibacy:

> Not unlike a wedding party, the arrangement at the altar that day consisted of my new friend flanked by his "sponsors" who dressed like groomsmen, ready to witness and celebrate their friend's promises before God to live a chaste life in service to the church. When I asked him why he did it, he spoke about not wanting to be a spiritual "lone ranger." He said he didn't want to drift through adulthood as if in a holding pattern; he didn't want to be defined by an absence or a negative appellation like "unmarried" or "unattached." He spoke about wanting instead to have a destination for his love (the parish), a vision for his

flourishing (community, friendship, hospitality), and a name for his vocation ("vowed celibate," unlike "single," is a designation with a Christian pedigree).[120]

Thus, whether to officially and sacramentally represent Christ's marriage to His people or to voluntarily commit to serving one's parish, celibacy is a vocation to which other readers may feel called. The church and the world need the witness you provide.

APPENDIX
How That Darn Article Shaped My Thinking

During my 1996 summer internship in Washington, D.C., my supervisor recommended that I read an article about marriage, sex, and procreation. As I recall, it was quite philosophically dense, with all sorts of technical definitions. In fact, it was published not in *Time*, *People* or even *Christianity Today*, but the *Georgetown Law Journal*.[121] I refer to it as "that darn article". The authors argued that artificial contraception is morally problematic because it *intentionally removes from the sex act one of its essential purposes: procreation*.[122]

I say "one of its essential purposes" because the sex act has more than one purpose. According to evolutionary biology, procreation is one of them; according to human experience, bonding or uniting a couple in love is another. A view that takes into account the integrity of the whole person holds that these purposes belong together. According to the article my supervisor recommended, what's problematic about artificial contraception is that the couple intentionally chooses to block one of those significant purposes.

Using a food analogy helps to make this point. One of the natural, built-in purposes of eating is providing the body with nutrients. If I consume a burger but then engage in purging, that act intentionally removes the nutritional purpose of eating. Similarly, the authors of that darn article held that wearing a condom or using an intra-uterine device (IUD) deliberately removes a significant, built-in purpose of sex. Contraception separates the pleasure of sex from the purpose of procreation, and pursues the former while deliberately blocking the latter.

Upon reading the article, I tracked the initial argument, but I kept coming back to a question: Can we say that, on days when a couple knows that fertility isn't possible, procreation remains one of the purposes of the sexual act? If a couple has sex after menopause, for example, does it still make sense to talk about each act being open to procreation as one of its purposes?

I uncovered two answers to that question. First, the article's authors claim that certain actions are defined, in part, by the natural purpose that their relevant bodily organs carry in themselves. For instance, a stomach is identified as a stomach because of the natural purpose it serves—i.e., the bodily function of digestion. The authors also hold that an organ's inherent purpose remains a reality regardless of whether its natural function is achieved in a particular instance.[123] That is, a stomach is still a stomach even if on certain occasions, like after eating bad Mexican food, the process of digestion isn't successfully completed. We continue to identify it as a stomach because we recognise that it is designed for that purpose. It is the *kind of organ* that typically achieves that end; when digestion does take place, it's because of the stomach. In philosophical language, this organ is *naturally oriented toward* digestion.

Pregnancy may not result every time couples have sex, but when it does, it's the result of the sexual organs. They are *the kind of organs* that typically achieve that function. One factor that naturally orients the genitalia toward procreation is that they deposit and receive sperm in the proximity of an ovum.[124] The fact that the sperm may not fertilise that ovum several hours later doesn't change the identity of those organs as sexual organs, just as an indigestible meal doesn't change the identity of a stomach on a particular night. That is, the inherent purpose that defines sexual organs remains a reality even if procreation doesn't occur. Even if a wife is past menopause or a husband is infertile for another reason, they can still unite in *the kind of act* that typically leads to procreation. They can still engage in what the authors call a *reproductive-type* act.[125]

In this way of thinking about a sex act, even if procreation is not a *possibility*, it remains a built-in, natural *purpose*. And it's morally problematic to intentionally separate out and block one of the sexual act's significant, intrinsic purposes.

The second answer has to do with distinguishing an act's natural, built-in *purpose* from the *motivation* for engaging in it. My supervisor helped me to think this through. An act's purpose—what it is designed or naturally oriented to achieve—isn't necessarily the primary motivating factor for those who choose to engage in it.

An infertile couple will not be motivated to have sex because they expect it to lead to pregnancy. Nor did I suspect, while reading the article for the first time, that that would be the case for my future wife and me. I had a hard time believing that, for sex to be moral and wholesome, we would have to intend or expect conception each time. If you think about it, women are typically only fertile 4-7 days a month; on the other days their bodies are *naturally* infertile. There are also other seasons during a woman's life when procreation isn't possible, including pregnancy, breastfeeding, and post-menopause. Thus, even though procreation is an intrinsic purpose of sex, the question isn't whether procreation can be expected to result from each act. For natural reasons alone, it won't. The question is whether the couple approaches each sex act in accord with or intentionally blocking that inherent purpose.

To return to the food-related example I mentioned earlier, one of the natural, built-in purposes of eating is providing the body with nutrients. But that's not necessarily the conscious reason I open the fridge late at night. "I need to supply my bodily systems with nutrients to enable them to function properly" isn't what's going through my head at that point. Rather, I eat because I have the munchies; I want to satisfy my hunger. It's a wonderful thing that our conscious desires can align with natural purposes that serve our well-being. Imagine what a drag it would be to have to eat food regularly if it wasn't a pleasurable experience. (It would be more like the chore of filling up a car with fuel.)

As I've noted, however, to intentionally purge after eating is morally problematic. That's an example of disconnecting one's motivating desires from a natural, healthy end—or severing a person's *wilful, decision-making* nature from his *bodily* nature. Or, in C. S. Lewis' analogy, that would be like mistaking the rejuvenating pleasure of a hotel for home.

Pleasure can certainly be a motivating factor for doing something, but the desire for it should not damage or impede human flourishing, which is perfected in self-giving love. Thus, if their sexual choices accord with the full giving of entire selves, couples don't have to intend or expect pregnancy in order to achieve the good of making love.

The article's authors conclude that contraception doesn't accord with the natural end of the sexual drive—the comprehensive union that it aims at by design. Contraception intentionally separates the pleasure of sex from the significant purpose of procreation and blocks the latter, even when a couple has sex on naturally infertile days. In contrast, a couple practicing NFP abstains from sex during days of fertility, so they don't engage in sex in a way that intentionally sterilises it. Each time they do choose to make love, they are able to enjoy the pleasures of sex while being open to all of its purposes. (As I discuss in Chapter 6, even during non-fertile seasons, remaining conscious of the procreative orientation of the sexual act can help it convey something very meaningful to a spouse. Although they may feel it in their hearts and speak it with words, contraception prevents couples from saying to each other, "full, free, fruitful, forever union" *with their bodies*.)

A Note On Practicing NFP

Unlike a few generations ago, today a conviction against artificial contraception is a minority view in the West. Nevertheless, I would recommend that all single women, and especially couples considering marriage, learn how a woman's fertility signs can identify ovulation. It's inexpensive and relatively easy to learn and to practice. At the very least, you'll likely gain a newfound appreciation for the wonders of the human body and how God created amazing things to happen within women to make pregnancy possible. Also, when you do want to get pregnant, you'll have a good idea of when during your cycle to try.

Learning to track your fertility signs is easier before you're sexually active. Female readers: if you're not yet married and/or sexually active, take advantage of the time you have now to practice discerning your signs. It will cost you little but could save you much stress and anxiety down the road.

Fortunately, Karin and I had about seven months before getting married for her to get comfortable with this method. During that time, she learned that the day of her ovulation occurs at slightly different times during her cycle (which is why it's unreliable for women simply to assume that it's always the same day—for example, the 14th day—after their period starts). She also recognised that the length of her cycle itself changes slightly from month to month. Tracking all this greatly eased our minds once we got married. For example, we didn't panic when Karin's period didn't start on the 28th day, for we had seen that happen several times during our engagement (a season during which we were not yet having sex).

If you're interested in what this might mean for you, an easy way to start is to use a fertility and/or period tracking app that develops the habit of monitoring your signs and cycle. Just make sure that, if you are sexually active and desire to avoid pregnancy, you ultimately make your decisions using a reliable method—like one of those mentioned in endnote 65—and receive official education and training in it.

ENDNOTES

1   The sunflower is the official state flower of Karin's home state. She bears much in common with the wild *helianthus*, which, according to the Kansas Legislature, is "hardy and conspicuous, of definite, unvarying and striking shape, easily sketched … ideally adapted for artistic reproduction … and is full of the life and glory of the past, the pride of the present, and richly emblematic of the majesty of a golden future". Kansas Legislature website, 2011-2012 Legislative Sessions, 2012 Statute, Chapter 73, Article 18, "State Flower and Floral Emblem", accessed on December 20, 2016, http://bit.ly/2gVATLm.

2   N. T. Wright, *The New Testament and the People of God (Christian Origins and the Question of God, Volume One)* (Minneapolis, MN: Fortress Press, 1992), 40.

3   Ibid.

4   Tom Wolfe, *I Am Charlotte Simmons* (New York: Picador, 2004). Although he provides a disclaimer that the book is not based on any real college, his fictitious "Dupont University"—which is a gothic wonderland nestled in North Carolina and home to a national championship basketball team—sounds a lot like Duke. (Guess where Wolfe's own daughter graduated two years before the book's publication?)

5   The mock study went viral in 2010. See Katharine Q. Seelye and Liz Robbins, "Duke Winces as a Private Joke Slips Out of Control", *The New York Times*, October 7, 2010, accessed November 30, 2016, http://nyti.ms/2fBzXQi.

6   John Corvino and Maggie Gallagher, *Debating Same-Sex Marriage* (New York: Oxford University Press, 2012), 14.

7   W. Bradford Wilcox, "The Evolution of Divorce", *National Affairs*, I (Fall 2009), accessed October 29, 2016, http://bit.ly/2gXkJWc.

8   Quoted in Jeffrey Slonim, "Chelsea Clinton Talks Kids She and Marc 'Hope to Have Someday'", *People*, updated September 23, 2016, accessed November 21, 2016, http://bit.ly/2gIdxwI (emphasis added).

9   Stanley Hauerwas, author of *Resident Aliens, A Community of Character,* and *Hannah's Child,* taught at the Duke Divinity School for many years and was named "America's Best Theologian" by *Time* magazine in 2001.

10   Alasdair MacIntyre, author of *After Virtue, Whose Justice? Which Rationality?*, and *Three Rival Versions of Moral Inquiry*, taught in Duke University's philosophy department for several years in the mid-1990s.

11   I've pulled together the threads of the ancient Jewish betrothal process from various sources, which are referenced in subsequent endnotes. For a summary account of this process, see Fred H. Wight, *Manners and Customs of Bible Lands* (Chicago: Moody Press, 1953), Chapter 14.

12   See Isaiah 61:10; Jeremiah 2:32.

13   See Song of Songs 3:11.

14   See Judges 14:12.

15   Compare that to the view one atheist skeptic articulated in an online article a few years ago. In commenting on the popular belief of newlyweds that they will always remain "in love", he notes that, "emotional responses such as love are really beyond our conscious control, we are really at their mercy. With this considered, it seems unlikely that a person could ever guarantee their undying love. They may very well intend to love another forever, but throughout their lives people change". Here love is clearly understood as an emotion that people feel prior to getting married. Because we cannot control this feeling, however, the author is forced to dismiss vows of permanent fidelity: "If ... two people found themselves in a loveless marriage, are we to suppose that due to their initial promise they will consequently have to remain within the relationship? No, such a view is not commonly held". See "Marriage, according to law in Australia, is the union of a man and a woman to the exclusion of all others voluntarily entered into for life", Young Australian Skeptics blog, September 27, 2010, accessed October 2, 2016, http://bit.ly/2fiXVQp.

16   You can get a sense of this from the King James Version, which translates the adjectives "patient" and "not self-seeking" as the verbs "suffereth long" and "seeketh not her own". Or read Anthony Thiselton's *The First Epistle to the Corinthians*, where he renders "patient" as "waits patiently", "kind" as "shows kindness", "not self-seeking" as "is not preoccupied with the interests of the self", and so forth. Anthony Thiselton, *The First Epistle to the Corinthians* (Grand Rapids, MI: Eerdmans Publishing, 2000), 1046.

17   C. S. Lewis identifies this as perhaps the original and primordial question facing human beings: What will we do with the gift we've been given of a "self"? You and I were each given a self at birth. As lovers, our selves are pointed toward some object: the object of our desires and affections. The question is, to whom or what will we give ourselves? Will we give ourselves to another person, or to God, or inward to an experience of self-pleasure, security, etc.? The Christian story suggests that what we were made for—our purpose in life—is to participate in relationships in which we give ourselves to God and others and receive the gift of God and others to us. "Whoever tries to keep their life will lose it, and whoever loses their life will preserve

it" (Luke 17:33). But giving our lives solely to the pursuit of our own good is an all-too-real possibility. "[T]he mere existence of a self—the mere fact that we call it 'me'—includes, from the first, the danger of self-idolatry", says Lewis. "Since I am I, I must make an act of self-surrender." C. S. Lewis, *The Problem of Pain* (New York: Collier Books, 1962), 81.

18 John Zizioulas provides a robust theological discussion of this point in his book *Being as Communion*. "There is no true being without communion. Nothing exists as an 'individual,' conceivable in itself ", he writes. "The person cannot exist without communion." John Zizioulas, *Being as Communion: Studies in Personhood and the Church* (Crestwood, NY: St Vladimir's Seminary Press, 1985), 18.

19 Brant Pitre, *Jesus the Bridegroom: The Greatest Love Story Ever Told* (New York: Image, 2014), 59.

20 Stanley Hauerwas, *A Community of Character: Toward a Constructive Christian Social Ethic* (Notre Dame, IN: University of Notre Dame Press, 1981), 284, note 26.

21 Even factors that are more "internal", like our memories or our own sense of self, cannot be entirely separated from our "external" relationships.

22 See Matthew 25:34-45.

23 It is worth thinking about the implications for the way God wants us to relate personally with Him. Does God call for a "personal relationship" that is at odds with His physical creation and our bodily nature? Or does He provide all sorts of material things with which to love and worship Him (water, wine, oil, wheat, hands to anoint others, colour to make paintings, stone to make sculptures, wood to make musical instruments)? Yes, we should guard against misusing and perverting material things, but the question is whether God created such things partly as means through which we can "voice creation's praise". See Jeremy Begbie, *Voicing Creation's Praise: Towards a Theology of the Arts* (Edinburgh: T&T Clark, 1991).

24 See Genesis 2:18.

25 Anthony Esolen, "Sanity & Matrimony: Ten Arguments in Defense of Marriage (Part 1 of 2)", *Touchstone* (July/August 2010), accessed September 3, 2016, http://bit.ly/2gXoISI.

26 Some people experience the tension of this divide within their own being—a condition known as gender dysphoria. For whatever reason, their psychological and emotional experience as a male or female conflicts with their biology and anatomy, which can lead to great distress. (Many youth suffering from gender dysphoria report that their conflict lessened over time or ceased entirely, but others experience this discomfort into adulthood.) Those of us who do not experience this tension between psychology and biology cannot imagine what it must be like, but we can try to listen and walk compassionately alongside those who do. As communities of truth and grace, churches need to help them carry the cross of responding faithfully

to this condition while providing the sort of communal body in which they feel they belong.

[27]   See Aristotle, *Parts of Animals*, trans. by A. L. Peck and E. S. Forster (Cambridge, MA: Harvard University Press, 1937), Book III, Part 3.

[28]   Lewis, *The Problem of Pain*, op. cit., 115. G. K. Chesterton makes a similar point: "Sex is an instinct that produces an institution ... That institution is the family ... Sex is the gate of that house; and romantic and imaginative people naturally like looking through a gateway. But the house is very much larger than the gate. There are indeed a certain number of people who like to hang about the gate and never get any further". G. K. Chesterton, *G.K.'s Weekly*, January 29, 1928. I was alerted to this quote by Glenn Stanton.

[29]   Some choose the route of sexual consumerism and resist any cultural limits to satisfying bodily impulses. But by repeatedly giving in to their urges, they risk becoming slaves to them. This is a risk for all of us. It's possible to get to the point where we can no longer control some of our desires; rather, they can begin to control us. Thus, we find a major irony of our times: in a culture fashioned on the premise of sexual freedom, we're enslaved to our own hormones!

[30]   Suppressing all physical touch before marriage has honourable goals, but it can also lead to unintended consequences. One is the temptation to think of sexual urges as something to be ashamed of. Lauren Winner, the author of *Real Sex*, notes that this can have negative consequences once a couple gets married: "Rather than spending our unmarried years stewarding and disciplining our desires, we ... persuade ourselves that the desires themselves are horrible. ... We spend years guarding our virginity, but find, upon getting married, that we cannot just flip a switch. Now that sex is licit, sanctioned—even blessed by our community—we are stuck with years of work (and sometimes therapy) to unlearn a gnostic anxiety about sex; to learn, instead, that sex is good". Lauren F. Winner, *Real Sex: The Naked Truth about Chastity* (Grand Rapids, MI: Brazos Press, 2005), 95. (While I cannot vouch for some of Winner's subsequent writings, I found *Real Sex* to be helpful in addressing these issues.)

[31]   Alasdair MacIntyre, *After Virtue: A Study in Moral Theory* (Second Edition) (Notre Dame, IN: University of Notre Dame Press, 1984), 216.

[32]   See Matthew 19:21. If money is inherently bad, Jesus would essentially be commanding greedy people to harm their neighbours by giving them something evil.

[33]   See Matthew 6:24.

[34]   This approach was reflected by Pope John Paul II in the early 1980s when advising that, "a progressive education in self-control of the will, of sentiments, of emotions ... must be developed from the simplest gestures, in which it is relatively easy to put the inner decision into practice". John Paul II, *Man and Woman He Created Them: A Theology of the Body*, trans. Michael Waldstein (Boston, MA: Pauline Books and Media, 2006), 644.

35   Influenced by the EPIC Story, many couples buy into the notion that marriage is based on the emotion of love, which they cannot help falling into and out of. Many of these couples, though, desire to celebrate their love by exchanging vows and making public promises. What sense, though, does it make to commit to a feeling that you can't control or to a relationship that you can easily break when you want? The noticeable difference that a promise makes seems to kick in precisely when the promise-maker no longer feels like keeping it—i.e., when the will needs to overrule the want. In marriage, spouses choose to bind themselves with an obligation that has authority even when their feelings, moods and desires change. That's the main point. But couples—and no-fault divorce laws—that base marriage on love-as-a-feeling essentially remove that kind of authority from the marriage commitment. In this context, the exchange of wedding vows essentially involves a *declaration to act in line with the way they feel for as long as they are "in love"*. But wouldn't they do that anyway—i.e., act in line with the way they feel—even without those vows? What does making a commitment add to the situation that is different from simply following their emotions? When those emotions fade, reason would seem to dictate that the two split; there would be no more love to commit to. Thus, we make with our spouse a meaningful commitment not to feelings of the heart but to acts of the will. The latter are within our power to control.

36   Michael P. Foley, "Betrothals: Their Past, Present, and Future", *Studia Liturgica* 33/1 (2003): 38.

37   Catherine Latimer and Michael J. McManus, "How to Give Marriage Insurance to Premarital Couples", 2001, Marriage Savers, Potomac, MD, accessed November 19, 2016, http://bit.ly/2gXntTh.

38   J. Robin Summers and Jo Lynn Cunningham, "Premarital Counseling by Clergy: a Key Link Between Church and Family", *Family Science Review* 2/4 (November 1989): 333.

39   Jennifer Gauvain, "The Shocking Truth for Thirty Percent of Divorced Women", *The Huffington Post*, August 6, 2011, updated October 6, 2011, accessed September 24, 2016, http://huff.to/2fP29xN.

40   Michael W. Goheen, *A Light to the Nations: The Missional Church and the Biblical Story* (Grand Rapids, MI: Baker Academic, 2011), 35.

41   Old Testament scholar Dennis J. McCarthy wrote, "there is no doubt that covenants, even treaties, were thought of as establishing a kind of quasi-familial unity". Dennis J. McCarthy, *Old Testament Covenant: A Survey of Current Opinions* (Richmond: Westminster John Knox Press, 1972), 33, quoted in Gordon P. Hugenberger, *Marriage as a Covenant: Biblical Law and Ethics as Developed from Malachi* (Eugene, OR: Wipf & Stock, 2014), 179. See also Scott W. Hahn, *Kinship by Covenant: A Canonical Approach to the Fulfillment of God's Saving Promises* (New Haven, CT: Yale University Press, 2009), esp. Chapters 1-2.

[42]   Paul Kalluveettil, *Declaration and Covenant: A Comprehensive Review of Covenant Formulae from the Old Testament and the Ancient Near East* (Rome: Biblical Institute Press, 1982), 212, quoted in Hugenberger, *Marriage*, op. cit., 179.

[43]   Wedding vows in the Presbyterian tradition, similar to the ones that Karin and I used, state, "I promise ... to be your loving and faithful wife/husband; in plenty and in want; in joy and in sorrow; in sickness and in health; as long as we both shall live. So help me God". See "Sample Wedding Vows", #15, St. Andrews Presbyterian Church, accessed November 25, 2016, http://bit.ly/2g9gCll. Also, vows in the Eastern Orthodox Church read, "I, ___, take you, ___, as my wedded wife/husband and I promise ... to be faithful to you, and not to forsake you until death do us part. So help me God, one in the Holy Trinity and all the Saints". Other traditions use phrases such as "in the name of God", "according to God's holy ordinance", and "before God and these witnesses". See "Traditional Wedding Vows From Various Religions", The Knot, accessed November 25, 2016, http://bit.ly/1LEKP95.

[44]   Chaim Reines, "Human Relationships in the Jewish Tradition", *Judaism*, 26/3 (Summer 1977): 364. For example, upon cutting a covenant with Laban, Jacob "invited his relatives to a meal" (Genesis 31:54). See also the meal that Moses, Aaron and other elders of Israel ate upon entering a covenant with Yahweh on Mt. Sinai (Exodus 24:11).

[45]   See John 13:2-5, 13-14.

[46]   See W. Bradford Wilcox et al, *Why Marriage Matters, Third Edition: 30 Conclusions from the Social Sciences* (West Chester, PA: Broadway Publications, 2011). For a summary of *Why Marriage Matters*, outlining the difference that marriage makes to children's physical health, mental health, economic well-being, educational achievement, criminal behaviour, and high-quality relationships with their parents, see http://bit.ly/2gXkhau. Also, David Popenoe, a sociologist at the University of Rutgers, says, "Few propositions have more empirical support in the social sciences than this one: compared to all other family forms, families headed by married, biological parents are best for children". Quoted in David Blankenhorn, *The Future of Marriage* (Reprint Edition) (New York: Encounter Books, 2009), 123.

[47]   Pitre, *Jesus the Bridegroom*, op. cit., 92-93.

[48]   Hauerwas, *A Community of Character*, op. cit., 282, note 14.

[49]   Lauren Sandler, "None is Enough", *Time* (August 12, 2013): 38-45.

[50]   See Psalm 127:3.

[51]   A possible biblical support for this claim is found in Malachi: "[T]he Lord is the witness between you and the wife of your youth. ... Has not the one God made you? You belong to [God] in body and spirit. And what does the one God seek? Godly offspring. So be on your guard, and do not be unfaithful to the wife of your youth" (2:14-15).

52   It's a common view in the modern West that the government should stay out of people's bedrooms. We may rightly ask why the law should impose regulations on our intimate *friendships* (relationships based on intimacy rather than procreation)—why, that is, the state should have the power to require official approval and paperwork to enter and leave them. In contrast, I'm suggesting that the state does have a valid and compelling reason to regulate relationships that typically bring about new citizens.

53   Bertrand Russell, *Marriage and Morals* (London: Allen & Unwin, 1929), 96.

54   Sherif Girgis, Ryan T. Anderson, and Robert P. George, *What Is Marriage?: Man and Woman: A Defense* (New York: Encounter Books, 2012), 96.

55   Leo Tolstoy, *Anna Karenina*, trans. by Rosamund Bartlett (Oxford: Oxford University Press, 2014), 454, 456.

56   Wendell Berry, *Sex, Economy, Freedom & Community* (New York: Pantheon Books, 1993), 119.

57   Winner, *Real Sex*, op. cit., 59-60.

58   These questions, from Dr. Neil Clark Warren's *Finding the Love of Your Life*, can be found at "50 Item List of Helpful Marriage Similarities", Family Life Education Institute, accessed October 29, 2016, http://bit.ly/2gXkkmG.

59   In August 1930, the Church of England became the first church to reverse course on the moral permissibility of marital contraception.

60   Pre-modern methods of contraception included douches concocted from various plants and herbs; pessaries—substances inserted into the vagina to block or kill sperm; and prophylactics fashioned from linen or animal intestines. See Megan L. Evans, "A desire to control: Contraception throughout the ages", *Historia Medicinae* (April 20, 2009), accessed November 28, 2016, http://www.medicinae.org/e08

61   The primary biblical text that bears on this issue is found in Genesis 38. According to an ancient Near Eastern custom known as the Law of the Levirate, if a married man died before having children, his brother had the responsibility to marry and have children by the widow. Onan's brother died, but when Onan married the widow Tamar and had sex with her, he withdrew and "spilled his semen on the ground to keep from providing offspring for his brother. What he did was wicked in the Lord's sight; so the Lord put him to death" (verses 9-10). Biblical scholars debate whether Onan's sin was violating the Levirate or practicing contraceptive behaviour. John Calvin held that Onan's sin was both his defrauding of his dead brother and his act of coitus interruptus. See John F. Kippley, *Sex and the Marriage Covenant: A Basis for Morality* (Second Edition) (San Francisco, CA: Ignatius Press, 2005), 325-331.

62   Yes, the Church believes that marriage should be open to children. But the Church also recognises that sometimes there are serious reasons to avoid getting pregnant. In such cases, human beings can exercise their God-given reason in determining when it's best to have children and how many to have. Parents should view children as a

gift, but they should also make responsible decisions as they grow their family. This can include the decision to avert pregnancy through approved means during certain seasons.

[63] The withdrawal method—i.e., the act performed by Onan as described in note 61 above—does not employ artificial materials; nevertheless, the Catholic Church deems it morally problematic because it intentionally removes a significant purpose of sex.

[64] Knowing what I know now, I'm a little surprised that the arguments in that darn article were enough to change my mind. After all, most of their weight seemed to rest on the philosophical definition of certain kinds of acts. That seemed pretty abstract and theoretical. Thus, although the rationale struck me as being accurate, I did not yet find it beautiful. That would come a little later in thinking about the role of sex within the story of covenant love. The following year, I would also add to this natural law argument a broader one concerning the shaping of moral character and community, and years later I would complement both of these arguments with a sacramental understanding of sex and the body. (See John Paul II, *Man and Woman*, op. cit.)

[65] This is one of several forms of natural family planning referred to as "Fertility Awareness Based Methods of Family Planning" or FABMs for short. The two that we are most familiar with are the Billings Ovulation Method (see www.woombinternational.org) and the Creighton Model (www.creightonmodel.com).

[66] In terms of NFP's effectiveness, I wonder how many of its reported "failures" have been due to the method itself or to the self-discipline of those practicing it. It's true that some women's cycles (especially those of athletes) are erratic and their signs are difficult to read. For many other cases, though, when determining when to have sex, couples simply cut it too close to the days when they're fertile.

[67] NFP creates a natural rhythm of anticipation and fulfilment, or fasting and feasting. As a couple goes through a period of abstaining from sex for a week or two, they tend to build up the desire for it. This absence makes the heart—as well as the entire body—grow fond for sexual union. Imagine intensely looking forward to sex every time you engage in it and you'll understand the hidden secret of NFP.

This isn't to say that practicing NFP is free from frustrations. Far from it. I noted earlier how there always seemed to be free food available on the Thursdays that we fasted in college; after we got married, business trips or illnesses always seemed to start on the first "safe" opportunity to have sex each month. Of course, practicing this approach to NFP can also be challenging for women whose signs are difficult to read or who are going through a season of stress or pre-menopause.

[68] This aspect of engagement is hard and requires great discipline. It's one reason why I favour short engagements, assuming the counselling takes place beforehand!

[69] Hauerwas, *Community of Character*, op. cit., 180.

70   Lauren Winner, who seems to accept artificial contraception, nevertheless writes, "if some of us opt to use contraception and others do not, we might all press some questions about the way birth control affects our understanding and practice of sexuality. ... The question we need to ask, I think, is what kind of sexual persons contraception invites us to be". Winner, *Real Sex*, op. cit., 65.

71   C. S. Lewis, *Mere Christianity* (New York: Harper San Francisco, 2001), 105.

72   Quoted in Hauerwas, *Community of Character*, op. cit., 282, note 14 (emphasis added).

73   Shared projects are extremely important in marriage, especially projects that pursue goods larger than the couple's own happiness. Indeed, one reason we're tempted to ground modern marriage in felt love, and evaluate it in terms of its ability to fulfil emotional needs, is because the family has lost its authority in most other public functions. Whereas the family used to be a primary centre for economic production, education, and health care, today these and other functions tend to be exercised by specialist, "public" institutions. As a result, the family has come to be viewed merely as a "private" institution—that is, a refuge where parents and children can escape the responsibilities of work and school. This has led one sociologist to describe the modern family as a "haven in a heartless world". As other family functions have decreased, expectations of personal intimacy, emotional intensity, and sexual chemistry have increased. See Hauerwas, *Community of Character*, op. cit., 158-165.

74   See Jeremiah 2:32.

75   Regarding this process, see Ellen Dooley, "Wedding Ceremonies in Ancient Palestine and the Wedding Feast of the Lamb", *Evangelical Journal* 26/2 (2008): 82.

76   See Exodus 28:31-32. Also, "For he has clothed me with garments of salvation and arrayed me in a robe of his righteousness, as a bridegroom adorns his head like a priest, and as a bride adorns herself with her jewels" (Isaiah 61:10-11).

77   Wight, *Manners and Customs*, op. cit., 130.

78   See the description in Psalm 45:10-15.

79   See Song of Songs 3:11. Couples married in the Byzantine Church still wear crowns during weddings, which are known as crowning ceremonies or "the mystery of crowning".

80   For the description of a similar carriage, see Song of Songs 3:9-10.

81   Dooley, "Wedding Ceremonies", op. cit., 82. One scholar reports the story of King Agrippa riding with his suite when they came upon a bridal procession. Supposedly, the King ordered his men to give way to them, declaring that, although he wore the crown always, they wore it only on that special day. Reines, "Human Relationships", op. cit., 365.

82   Wight, *Manners and Customs,* op. cit., p. 132.

[83]   See Matthew 24:1-14.

[84]   See Psalm 19:4-5.

[85]   Scott Hahn, *The Lamb's Supper: The Mass as Heaven on Earth* (New York: Doubleday, 1999), 125.

[86]   Deuteronomy 22:13-19 reads, "If a man takes a wife and, after sleeping with her, dislikes her and slanders her and gives her a bad name, saying, 'I married this woman, but when I approached her, I did not find proof of her virginity,' then the young woman's father and mother shall bring to the town elders at the gate proof that she was a virgin. Her father will say to the elders, 'I gave my daughter in marriage to this man, but he dislikes her. Now he has slandered her and said, "I did not find your daughter to be a virgin." But here is the proof of my daughter's virginity.' Then her parents shall display the cloth before the elders of the town, and the elders shall take the man and punish him. They shall fine him a hundred shekels of silver and give them to the young woman's father, because this man has given an Israelite virgin a bad name. She shall continue to be his wife; he must not divorce her as long as he lives". (It should be noted that, not only can slight bleeding during sex be caused by factors other than the hymen breaking, but also the hymen can stretch or tear for reasons other than sexual intercourse.)

[87]   See Genesis 29:27-28 and Judges 14:12, 17.

[88]   Hauerwas, *Community of Character*, op. cit., 181, 281-282.

[89]   Hugenberger, *Marriage as a Covenant*, op. cit., 251.

[90]   Gergis et al, *What is Marriage?*, op. cit., 113, note 6.

[91]   See the Appendix for the distinction between an act's *purpose* and what *motivates* it.

[92]   These lines, taken from *The Book of Common Prayer*, are listed as sample vows on the popular website The Knot under "Protestant wedding ceremony script". Accessed November 22, 2016, http://bit.ly/2gKML4c.

[93]   Those of us who don't experience same-sex attraction cannot imagine what it's like to live with this reality. We can, however, do our best to listen, love, and learn from those who do. We would also do well to remember that the church is a community of sexual beings who all, in one form or another, struggle in living out God's intentions for sex and marriage. We need to help each other carry the various crosses that we've been given to bear, whether it's living in singleness (for someone who wants to get married), remaining married (for someone who has fallen into infatuation with someone other than their spouse), or refraining periodically from sex (for a couple who may need to avoid additional pregnancy). The church should strive to welcome all who are struggling to remain faithful to God in their sexuality. (See the Afterword towards the end of this book.)

[94]   I wonder if one reason why so many Christians today have trouble providing

a coherent stance regarding the question of same-sex marriage is because they themselves have adopted a contraceptive mentality—i.e., a mentality that severs the intrinsic connection between sex and procreation. For contracepting opposite-sex couples as well as same-sex couples, sexual acts do not *intrinsically* say, "I hereby give myself fully to you in the way that brings forth new life to love". The fact that such acts are not ordered toward procreation means that they do not bring the will into alignment with the natural orientation of the sexual drive: full, comprehensive self-giving love across all dimensions of a human person. They are thus not the kind of acts that consummate and renew marriage.

95   This is one reason why rape does not consummate a marriage.

96   To the extent that masturbation relies upon porn, it comes under the same critique. Furthermore, we can also assess masturbation in terms of the earlier claims in this chapter that sex is 1) a way for spouses to say something to each other through their bodies, and 2) an act of the whole person—not just one aspect of him/her. Individual masturbation doesn't seem to say anything to or forge a connection with someone else; nor does it treat oneself as a full, integrated person who is more than their capacity to experience pleasure. As my friend Matthew Lee Anderson notes, objectifying another person in pornography or mental fantasies—which is often involved with masturbation—has a similar effect on oneself: "we treat our *[own]* bodies as machines … as instrument[s] for personal pleasure and gratification. Human sexuality is inherently social, and masturbation is not". Matthew Lee Anderson, *Earthen Vessels: Why Our Bodies Matter to our Faith* (Minneapolis, MN: Bethany House, 2011), 133, 135 (emphasis added). For a variety of Christian views on masturbation, see Rachel Held Evans, "Christians & Masturbation: Seven Perspectives", Rachel Held Evans Blog, June 3, 2013, accessed November 22, 2016, http://bit.ly/1h16Bl1.

97   Again, the word *apokalypsis* literally means "unveiling", an act that took place in the Jewish Betrothal Story immediately before consummation.

98   There are various recurring themes and images (agricultural, judicial, familial, royal, military, etc.) that help interpret scriptural phrases and events. And, of course, certain significant actions like the Last Supper can be understood through more than one interpretive lens. I'm suggesting that divine marriage, while not the only image, is an especially powerful one for making sense of many key moments in the biblical story. In particular, this image draws out the personal nature, family-expanding orientation, and faithfulness of God's love.

99   It is worth noting the significance of the fact that the Abrahamic covenant was sealed on the male sexual organ—i.e., the organ used to expand families and consummate marriage covenants. Yahweh asked Abraham to cut the part of the body through which His promise to provide numerous descendants would be fulfilled. Moreover, God designated circumcision as the way to identify male membership in the covenant people. Not only did this dramatise the curse of being "cut off" from this people upon breaking the covenant, but it also resulted in blood, the typical means of sealing

covenants. When a husband and wife consummated their marriage sexually, bleeding also typically resulted, this time from the woman. See Hugenberger, *Marriage as a Covenant*, op. cit., 196; John Goldingay, "The Significance of Circumcision", *Journal for the Study of the Old Testament* 88 (2000): 8-9.

[100] See also Isaiah 61:10-11.

[101] Also, "The Lord had said to Abram, 'Go from your country, your people and your father's household to the land I will show you. I will make you into a great nation, and I will bless you; I will make your name great, and you will be a blessing. I will bless those who bless you, and whoever curses you I will curse; and all peoples on earth will be blessed through you'" (Genesis 12:1-3).

[102] Jeremiah 3:8 states that Yahweh gave Israel a "certificate of divorce". Scholars disagree on whether this line conveys a warning or a completed action. It seems that Yahweh somehow suspended communion with Israel publically and "sent her away" (verse 8) from His presence while nevertheless remaining faithful to their covenant bond. He calls her in verse 12 to "return", and in verse 14 (which comes *after* the sentence about a certificate of divorce) He declares to Israel, "I am married to you" (NKJV). Thus, for the purposes of this book, we can assert that, although separated for a time, Yahweh didn't renounce His love for Israel, nor did He renege on His marriage covenant with her.

[103] See also Ezekiel 36:27-28: "And I will put my Spirit in you and move you to follow my decrees and be careful to keep my laws. Then you will live in the land I gave your ancestors; you will be my people, and I will be your God" and Zechariah 8:8: "I will bring them back to live in Jerusalem; they will be my people, and I will be faithful and righteous to them as their God".

[104] Pitre, *Jesus the Bridegroom*, op. cit., 66. Pitre links Jesus telling the Samaritan woman that she has had five husbands to the fact that the Samaritan peoples had worshipped five male deities throughout their history. (2 Kings 17:24 and 33 read, "The king of Assyria brought people from Babylon, Kuthah, Avva, Hamath and Sepharvaim and settled them in the towns of Samaria to replace the Israelites. They took over Samaria and lived in its towns. ... [These five national groups] worshiped the Lord, but they also served their own gods in accordance with the customs of the nations from which they had been brought".) According to Pitre, "Amazingly, the male gods of the Samaritans were actually called 'Baals'—the Canaanite word for 'husbands' or 'lords' (see Hosea 2:16). ... the Samaritans also worshipped a sixth deity: YHWH, the God of Israel". Thus, Jesus' statement to the Samaritan woman, "you have had five husbands, and he whom you now have is not your husband" (John 4:18) is a reference to YHWH. In other words, in this encounter at a well, Jesus "is initiating the time when the people of Samaria will be incorporated into the new Israel by being united to the true Bridegroom: YHWH, the living God of Israel" (67-68).

[105] See Scott Hahn, *A Father Who Keeps His Promises: God's Covenant Love in Scripture* (Cincinnati, OH: Servant Books, 1998), 225-233.

[106] Interview with J. John, quoted in Matthew Schmitz, "N. T. Wright on Gay Marriage", *First Things* (June 11, 2014), accessed October 8, 2016, http://bit.ly/2fDXAWL.

[107] Scott Hahn notes that the Hebrew word for swearing an oath or "cutting a covenant" (*sheba*) was based on the word for the number seven. Thus, to swear a covenant oath in ancient Israel literally meant to "seven oneself". Hahn, *A Father*, op. cit., 51.

Sheba is also closely related to the Hebrew word meaning *full* or *complete*. Fittingly, in Scripture the number seven is a symbol of covenant fullness or completeness. The creation story, as told in Genesis, has a sevenfold structure, with the first verse consisting of exactly seven words in Hebrew (Genesis 1:1). God designated the seventh day of creation as the Sabbath, marking it as "a lasting covenant" with creation (Exodus 31:16). Noah took seven pairs of every kind of clean animal on the ark to sacrifice (Genesis 7:2). When Abraham swore a covenant oath with Abimelech at Beersheba (literally meaning the well (Beer) of the oath (*Sheba*)), he used seven lambs (Genesis 21:28-31). When God called Moses to climb Mt. Sinai, He covered the mountain with a cloud for six days and then called Moses to enter the cloud on the seventh day (Exodus 24:15-18). Moses commanded the priests and elders of Israel to read the Law to the people every seven years (Deuteronomy 31:9-11). When David had the ark of the covenant brought to the City of David, the priests sacrificed seven bulls and seven rams (1 Chronicles 15:25-26). The Temple that King Solomon built took seven years to complete (1 Kings 6:38). In the book of Revelation, God's heavenly temple is opened after seven angels sound seven trumpets (Revelation 8-11). The Jewish faith celebrates seven holy festivals (unleavened bread, Pentecost, Sabboth, Passover, Roshashana, Yom Kippur, and Booths (*Sukkot*)), and the Catholic Church identifies seven sacraments (Baptism, Eucharist, Confirmation, Reconciliation, Anointing of the sick, Marriage, and Holy orders). Noting all these occurrences of the number seven can help us appreciate how central a role the theme of covenant plays in the Christian story.

[108] As missiologist Lesslie Newbigin argued, "They are chosen not for themselves, not to be the exclusive beneficiaries of God's saving work, but to be the bearers of the secret of his saving work for the sake of all. They are chosen to go and bear fruit. ... To be elect in Christ Jesus ... means to be incorporated into his mission to the world, to be the bearer of God's saving purpose for his whole world ..." Lesslie Newbigin, *The Gospel in a Pluralist Society* (Grand Rapids, MI: Eerdmans Publishing Company, 1989), 86-87.

[109] For similar expressions of this feeling, see Nicolas DiDomizio, "11 Brutally Honest Reasons Why Millennials Don't Want Kids", Connections.Mic, July 30, 2015, accessed November 30, 2016, http://bit.ly/2gTTcoK.

[110] "A child represents our willingness to go on in the face of difficulties, suffering, and the ambiguity of modern life and is thus our claim that we have something worthwhile to pass on. ... And marriage ... is a sign that we are a community sustained by hope." Hauerwas, *Community of Character*, op. cit., 165, 193.

[111] See 2 Peter 1:4.

[112] See Trent Dalton, "Date night", *The Weekend Australian* Magazine (November 5-6, 2016), accessed November 11, 2016, http://bit.ly/TinderAge.

[113] See James K. A. Smith, *Desiring the Kingdom: Worship, Worldview, and Cultural Formation* (Grand Rapids, MI: Baker Academic, 2009) and his more accessible *You Are What You Love: The Spiritual Power of Habit* (Grand Rapids, MI: Brazos Press, 2016).

[114] In *Betrothals: Their Past, Present, and Future,* Michael Foley points to examples of engagement/betrothal practices in modern times. For instance, in 1984 the Catholic Church first suggested a rite of engagement called the "Order for the Blessing of an Engaged Couple", which is intended to take place in the families' homes (p. 50). Maronite Catholics as well as practitioners of the West Syrian and Armenian rites still maintain a rite of betrothal, or "covenant", which includes a blessing of rings and wedding garments. According to Foley, in the East Syrian rite, marriage crowns are also blessed, along with an unconsecrated chalice of wine, a ring, and a cross (p. 56). The marriage ceremony of Eastern and Orthodox Churches is referred to as the "Mystery of Crowning". Foley, "Betrothals", op. cit.

[115] What Oliver O'Donovan says regarding homosexuality can, I think, be said about any of the factors mentioned in this section: "[It] is not the determining factor in any human being's existence; therefore it cannot be the determining factor in the way we treat a human being, and should not be the determining factor in the way a human being treats him- or herself". Oliver O'Donovan, *Church in Crisis: The Gay Controversy and the Anglican Communion* (Eugene, OR: Cascade Books, 2008), 105.

[116] In his article "Jigs for Marriage and Celibacy", Wesley Hill describes his experience of both married couples and singles offering "on-call love" and hospitality to others by, among other things, inviting them into their homes and sharing meals with them. See Wesley Hill, "Jigs for Marriage and Celibacy", *Comment* (November 24, 2016), accessed November 29, 2016, http://bit.ly/2fKjip0.

[117] Timothy Keller, *The Meaning of Marriage: Facing the Complexities of Commitment with the Wisdom of God* (New York: Dutton, 2011), 196. Remember that both Jesus and St. Paul were single their entire lives, showing that abundant life cannot hinge upon marriage. For good reflections on singleness from a Christian perspective, see also Hauerwas, *Community of Character*, op. cit., 189-191, and Jennifer A. Marshall, *Now and Not Yet: Making Sense of Single Life in the Twenty-First Century* (Colorado Springs, CO: Multnomah Books, 2007).

[118] Oliver O'Donovan, *Resurrection and Moral Order: An Outline for Evangelical Ethics* (Grand Rapids, MI: Eerdmans, 1986), 70.

[119] On the inside of Karin's and my wedding rings are inscribed the words "FOR AND UNTIL CHRIST".

[120] Hill, "Jibs for Marriage and Celibacy", op. cit.

[121] Gerard V. Bradley and Robert P. George, "Marriage and the Liberal Imagination", *Georgetown Law Journal* 84 (1995): 301-320.

[122] By "sex act" I'm referring specifically to the kind of act that typically results in procreation. There are, of course, more technical terms, like conjugal act, generative act, genital intercourse, coitus, mating, and so forth. I, however, will use the term "sex act" to describe the unique act in which a male and female combine to procreate.

[123] Ibid., 312.

[124] Of course, other bodily factors than genitalia are involved in sex. For example, the release of certain chemicals (like oxytocin) in the brain bond sexual partners emotionally and help create a feeling of belonging and devotion to each other and any children they may conceive. Thus, beyond just the genitals, we can say that the entire sexual drive—which includes the will and certain neurological functions—is naturally oriented to a unitive and procreative one-flesh union, and remains so even during seasons when fertility isn't naturally possible.

[125] Ibid., 311-313. For a more recent presentation of this argument, see Gergis et al, *What is Marriage?*, op. cit., 23-28.

ACKNOWLEDGEMENTS

The contents of this book were developed during my time in both the United States and Australia. I'm thankful for students, friends, and colleagues in both countries who listened, discussed, and contributed to my understanding of these issues. Smaller conversations with various university student groups as well as larger presentations to conference and retreat audiences were invaluable in honing the narrative I tell in these pages. A special thanks to students at the Millis Institute in Brisbane for their candid conversations about sex and marriage, and for their countercultural commitment to pursue the good, true, and beautiful through studying the liberal arts.

I am greatly indebted to the many teachers and authors who have shaped my thinking over the years. Many of them, from C. S. Lewis, Stanley Hauerwas, and Oliver O'Donovan to Robert George, Scott Hahn, and John Paul II, are referenced in this book, but their influence has been much broader than even I am aware.

Several friends were kind enough to read the entire manuscript and make valuable comments, including Dave Benson, Peter Pellicaan, Glenn Stanton, Mark Makowiecki, Robert van Gend, Sally Vest, Alexandra Crook, Greg Fleming, Josh Good and John Inazu. Scott Cleveland and Allan Poole also read sections and gave helpful feedback.

My kids, Joshua, Christopher, and Katie were wonderful encouragers along the way, and they put up with a lot of dinner conversations about marriage and books lying around the house about theologies of sex. They also have endured an international move and been an active, faithful part of the Christ-centred collegiate learning communities I've helped to lead. Most of all, I appreciate the support, advice, patience, grace, and editing assistance provided by my Kansas sunflower, Karin. She helped weed out a lot of "Ryanisms" and has made this book—and my life—much better. I love you, Karin; thank you for sharing your story, identity and love with me.

ABOUT THE AUTHOR

DR RYAN MESSMORE directs the Millis Institute, a Christ-centred, tertiary liberal arts program that he designed at Christian Heritage College in Brisbane, Australia (www.millis.edu.au). He has also served as President of Campion College (Sydney) and a research fellow at the Heritage Foundation (Washington, D.C.). After receiving his bachelor's degree at Duke University and Masters of Theological Studies at Duke Divinity School, Ryan pursued an M.Phil. at Cambridge University and a D.Phil. at Oxford University (on the Trinity and political theology). He and his wife, Karin, live with their three kids in Brisbane, where they are still loyal watchers of Duke basketball games and where they teach their students (among other things) ballroom dancing. For more visit www.ryanmessmore.com.

Printed in Australia
AUOC01n0837130217
282990AU00002B/2/P

9 781925 501384